EASY, AFFORDABLE
RAW

For Jessica, Michael, Alexandria, Ledger, and Carter. I love you.

© 2014 Quarry Books
Text © 2014 Lisa Viger

First published in the USA in 2014
by Quarry Books, a member of
Quarto Publishing Group USA Inc.
100 Cummings Center
Suite 406-L
Beverly, MA 01915-6101
www.quarrybooks.com

Visit www.QuarrySPOON.com and help
us celebrate food and culture one spoonful
at a time!

18 17 16 15 14   1 2 3 4 5
ISBN: 978-1-59253-929-1
Digital edition published in 2014
eISBN: 978-1-62788-041-1
Library of Congress
Cataloging-in-Publication Data available

Cover and book design by Laura McFadden
Photography by Lisa Viger
Printed and bound in China

The information in this book is for
educational purposes only. It is not intended
to replace the advice of a physician or
medical practitioner. Please see your health
care provider before beginning any new
health program.

EASY, AFFORDABLE
RAW

*How to go raw on $10 a day
by the author of the blog
Raw on $10 a Day (or Less)*

LISA VIGER

Quarry Books
100 Cummings Center, Suite 406L
Beverly, MA 01915

quarrybooks.com • quarryspoon.com

Contents

Mixed Fruit Tart, page 153

Foreword

by Penni Shelton

I began my journey with healing foods nearly a decade ago when I found myself at the end of my rope physically, mentally, and spiritually. Lifelong battles with irritable bowel syndrome, allergies, asthma, chronic fatigue, headaches, PMS, eczema, weight, and post-traumatic stress had taken their toll on me. After having not found true wellness or recovery through the best efforts of Western medicine, I began to explore other healing modalities to see if there could be some relief outside of my well-meaning doctor's office walls.

It was a long road of discovery, but I eventually stumbled upon the very simple and common-sense teachings of raw food, and how eating a diet rich in real food could begin to bring a person's body into balance, better health, renewed energy, and authentic wholeness. With nothing to lose, I jumped into this new way of eating with both feet.

Within a very short period of time, my symptoms began to lessen and ultimately fade away. My skin began to clear, as did my mind. My energy began to return, and my breathing became effortless. The mucus that lined my digestive and respiratory tract began to expel, and the body fat began to gently release as I enjoyed eating a very simple diet of fruits, vegetables, and some nuts, seeds, and sprouts. How could it be that a simple change in my diet could yield such impressive results in such a short period of time?

One of the things I learned is that the diet I had grown up on wasn't real food at all. As a matter of fact, the foods and drinks that had comforted me since early childhood had actually created many of the health conditions I was suffering from. Sure the hamburgers, french fries, and sodas tasted pretty good, but they were also heavily laced with addictive chemicals, hydrogenated oils, pesticides, antibiotics, hormones, and other flavor-enhancing additives that were being created in high-tech laboratories, far away from the farmlands of our grandparents. Fast food has become a scary industrial commodity that is no longer serving us as a culture. Crops grown with genetically-modified organisms (GMOs), microwave ovens, Styrofoam containers, and the pain and suffering of innocent animals: The list goes on and on, and there is nothing sustainable or life-giving to any of it.

My passion for real food and getting back to our roots with eating is something that author Lisa Viger and I very much share. In my time as a health educator and wellness advocate, I've been bombarded by critics who say that eating a diet rich in raw and living foods is elitist and too expensive for ordinary people and that it's just a trend for hip foodies and "crunchy" bohemians. I have an altogether different perspective on it, because I believe that eating in this way is the oldest diet on the planet, and a return to real food for the mainstream eater is necessary and long overdue to help save our health and that of this planet.

Introduction: My Story

I first heard about raw foods about ten years ago in an online forum. The idea was to eat foods just as they were. What a brilliant and radical concept.

At the time, I was living in complete opposition to that ideal. I was overweight and living on restaurant food much of the time. I drank soft drinks almost every day, and I smoked cigarettes. My cholesterol was high, I had chronic sinus problems, I used antibiotics and pain relievers often, I had digestive issues, and I just didn't feel well most of the time.

I wasn't even forty years old, and in every way possible, I was a health disaster. To make matters worse, I was spending a small fortune to be that unhealthy. Had I continued that way, it would have cost even more in medical bills. And who can put a price on lost health?

I was so fresh-food challenged that when I first heard about raw foods, all of the food in my house was in cans or packages—except a head of cabbage and some potatoes. Then I became aware of the possibility of change, and I knew I could take a different course.

One of the first things I did was quit smoking. The health benefits from that have been enormous, and there are financial benefits, too. I save about $3,000 (€ 1,790) each year on cigarettes. Plus, I will probably eliminate lots of health care costs down the road.

The Book That Changed My Life

Then I read *The World Peace Diet* by Will Tuttle, Ph.D. It tied everything together: the way we use animals, how that's connected to how we treat our fellow human beings and the planet, and how that affects us physically, spiritually, and emotionally. Right away, I became vegan, and I have been vegan ever since.

The surprising thing is, I enjoy food more than I ever have. It's the opposite of deprivation. I can actually taste and smell things again, like I did when I was a kid. Remember when you were a kid and everything was so vibrant? Tastes, smells, and even vision were incredibly intense. That's how I feel now. Everything is brighter and more alive.

I'm fifty years old now, and since becoming always vegan and mostly raw, I've lost weight, my skin feels good, my cholesterol is in the healthiest range, I have no pains, and I am nearly always happy. I never feel the need for an afternoon nap. I sleep like a rock, and I wake refreshed. My digestion is excellent, and I'm stronger and more flexible than I remember being in my twenties. Not only that, but I'm saving money and living a more economical life now.

Living Raw on $10 a Day (or Less)

I started my blog, *Raw on $10 a Day (or Less)*, a few years ago, after hearing one too many times that healthy food is too expensive. My goal was to see how much it costs to eat healthy raw and vegan foods. I found it wasn't all that expensive or difficult to eat fresh, whole foods. I live in the country with only one local grocery store. I buy almost everything I need at that one store, with only a few exceptions for things such as cacao powder. Fresh produce is less expensive than most packaged and processed foods, and it's more economical than restaurant meals.

Raw foods are usually thought of as expensive and difficult to prepare, requiring exotic ingredients and pricey equipment. However, raw foods really are affordable. For the recipes in this book, I've used ingredients found in most local groceries. The chocolate-making supplies and few specialty ingredients used can be found in most health food stores and/or online.

I haven't used many superfoods or exotic ingredients, except for the chocolate chapter. I wanted a practical approach and common ingredients that would work for the experienced raw fooder, as well as the less experienced and those just getting started in living foods. Anyone who is concerned about both the quality of their food and the health of their wallet will enjoy *Easy, Affordable Raw*.

Making New Habits

The longer I was vegan and mostly raw, the easier it all became. After a few weeks of buying new things and eating in a different way, it became as habitual as anything else. Be aware that you're making new habits, and it will get easier over time. It won't be a struggle or an effort forever. In just a few weeks, your new lifestyle will be as habitual as your old one.

Today, I continue to feel fantastic and enjoy the physical and mental benefits of raw foods. I know that in the future I'll always be vegan and mostly raw and can't imagine going back to eating conventionally again.

As you begin to eat raw, I hope you have fun and can be joyful. Raw, fresh plant foods are incredibly joyful. They're beautiful, life-giving, healthy, and easy on the planet.

Part I

Starting Your Raw Journey

chapter

1

> **"**Man seeks to change the foods available in nature to suit his tastes, thereby putting an end to the very essence of life contained in them.**"** *—Sai Baba*

Why Raw?

A raw food diet is centered on fresh, uncooked fruits, vegetables, nuts, and seeds. It's unprocessed, unaltered, and, ideally, organic. The foods can be heated, but not above a certain temperature. Usually, the upper limit is about 118°F (48°C). After heating foods above that temperature, some nutrients can be changed or diminished, proteins begin to alter, and enzymes are lost.

Raw plant foods can be easy to prepare, as well as beautiful and delicious. The colors are vibrant and attractive. Raw food is naturally juicy, wet, and plump. Raw foods, such as those in the recipes in this book, will tantalize your taste buds and make your mouth water. They can be used to create decadent dishes that seem too good to be healthy.

Eating raw foods offer tremendous benefits to both your health and the environment.. This chapter will discuss some of the reasons you might consider a raw food lifestyle.

Raw Foods Are Sun Powered

We're all powered by sunlight. Every one of us gets our energy from the sun. Sound fanciful or impossible? Let me explain.

The sun is the ultimate energy source for all living organisms. Sunlight on green leaves begins the process of photosynthesis, which is how carbohydrates are created within the leaves of plants. Carbohydrates are the energy source of all living things. They fuel the life processes of the plant and continue to fuel the life processes of the being that eats the plant. When we eat green leaves, and the nuts and fruits that are grown on the plant with energy provided by green leaves, we are eating as close to the original source of energy—as close to the sun—as possible. This is the most efficient and economical way to obtain energy. The fewer steps we take away from the sun, the less waste there will be.

Raw Foods Are as Nature Intended

We're intended to eat fresh food, get lots of movement and lots of exercise, breathe lots of fresh air, enjoy the sun, be close to the earth, love our friends and family, and be happy and joyful. The further we get away from that ideal—and no one gets it perfect—the more physical and emotional health problems we have. Those are the things that will give us the best health whether our own individual concern is immune support or cancer prevention or weight loss or hormonal balance or bone health. Whatever the concern, whatever brings us to the place where we want to take action is connected to everything else. I don't think one condition can be separated from the rest of the body. The human body is a system, and everything works together and synergistically, not in isolation. The idea that there is a pill for this condition, or a supplement for that one, is limited. I think we have to nourish every part of our bodies and every part of our lives. It's about balance and connection.

Raw Food Tastes Better

Tasting as you go is important when making recipes using only fresh foods. If you buy a brand-name packaged cookie, you know exactly what you're getting. One of the reasons we use all those chemicals in food is to ensure uniformity.

Nature, on the other hand, is not uniform. One tomato is going to taste differently from another, and flavors are going to be stronger, milder, sweeter, or more bitter, depending on the individual ingredients.

Raw Food Contains More Nutrients

Plant foods are incredibly nutrient dense. They contain high amounts of important vitamins, minerals, and phytochemicals, as well as fiber, which is essential for effective digestion. At the same time, raw foods are low in calories, so there's less of a need to restrict food when you want to lose weight. Eating raw food can help make you feel fantastic, too. Here are some of the elements that contribute to its healthiness.

Enzymes: Virtually every living thing contains enzymes. We rely on enzymes for many vital chemical reactions that make life possible. There are more than 2,500 kinds of enzymes found in living things, and all are proteins. Because many are destroyed by heat, raw foods contain more enzymes than conventional foods. Some of the enzymes survive the digestive process, but not many. Not to worry, the human body is very good at making its own enzymes and doesn't ever run out.

Vitamins: Vitamins are organic compounds that are necessary for proper nutrition and growth. They cannot be synthesized in the body and so must be obtained from the diet. Because some vitamins are destroyed by heat, a raw food diet protects the vitamin content of what we eat.

Minerals: Minerals are naturally occurring inorganic solids. They're also necessary for proper nutrition, growth, and function and must be obtained from the diet. Some minerals that we need are calcium, selenium, iron, zinc, potassium, magnesium, and sodium. Because heat can also destroy or alter minerals, a raw food diet protects the mineral content in the foods we eat.

Antioxidants: Oxidation in the body damages cell membranes, proteins, lipids, and even DNA. It can cause acceleration of the aging process, heart disease, and cancers and also damage nerve cells in the brain leading to Alzheimer's disease and Parkinson's disease, and deterioration of the lens in the eye, which can cause blindness. Antioxidants prevent oxidation and oxidative stress and the damage it can cause in the body. The best sources of antioxidants are raw fruits and vegetables.

Phytonutrients: Phytonutrients are substances found in plants that can be beneficial to human health. Commonly known phytonutrients include beta-carotene, lycopene, and chlorophyll. Fruits and vegetables are concentrated sources of phytonutrients, and often it is phytonutrients that give fruit, and berries their distinctive colors. But not all phytonutrients are colorful: onions, garlic, and leeks have phytonutrients that aren't colorful. Because heat can destroy some phytonutrients, and this diet depends so heavily on fruits and vegetables, a raw food diet will contain far more phytonutrients than a conventional one.

Fiber: There are two types of fiber, soluble fiber and insoluble fiber. Both are essential for human health. Fiber moves wastes out of the body. Fruits and vegetables are rich in both kinds of fiber. Fiber isn't affected much by heat, so raw foods don't contain more fiber than cooked foods. However, when you eat a raw, plant-based diet, you'll be eating more fiber than most people, who fall woefully short.

And more? We've only barely scratched the surface of what we know about food and nutrition. Scientists discover new nutrients all the time, and in addition to the nutrients we know, such as vitamin C, niacin, and antioxidants, plants have literally thousands of nutrients we have yet to discover. Then there are the interactions and synergistic relationships between nutrients we're only beginning to understand and that have almost infinite combinations and possibilities. We know that fruits and vegetables are essential to human health. And we know the vitamins and minerals we need for optimal health are found in fresh produce.

Raw Foods Benefit Health

Eating more raw foods, and more fruits and vegetables in general, can have many health benefits, including the following.

Weight loss: Lower calories and higher nutritional content is a win-win situation for the body, with weight loss being one possible result. Fresh fruits and vegetables are water-rich. Some, such as watermelon, are as much as 90 percent water. This means they're very low in calories. They're also high in fiber, which helps regulate appetite and moves waste quickly through the body. All this can aid in weight loss.

Boosted energy: Cooked foods, especially of animal origin, can be heavy and require a great deal of energy to digest. This can leave us feeling sapped and depleted. By abstaining from the foods that reduce energy, and ensuring proper nutrition and proper hydration with a fresh, plant-based diet, your energy levels can increase.

Increased immunity: Vitamins, minerals, and other phytonutrients are vital to a healthy immune system. Most people know that vitamin C boosts immunity, but so do the B vitamins, including folic acid. Vitamin A deficiency impairs T-cell activity, vitamin E supports a healthy inflammatory response, and the mineral zinc is a potent immunostimulant. Omega-3 fatty acids, such as those found in flax and chia seeds, fight inflammation and help prevent autoimmune dysfunction and disease. Not only that, but it's thought that the aging of the immune system, which can leave the elderly vulnerable to influenza and pneumonia, can be reduced or prevented by eating enough fruits and vegetables.

Balanced hormones: One of the biggest advantages of any plant-based diet is that it eliminates animal products, which contain many naturally occurring hormones. Dairy products naturally contain high levels of estrogen, for example, and are linked to hormonal cancers such as breast and prostate. In countries where there is low consumption of animal products, there is also a low incidence of PMS and menopausal symptoms and lower rates of breast and prostate cancers.

Smoother, clearer skin: Most acne is caused by an underlying sensitivity to certain hormones. For some people, any variation from the hormonal ideal will cause a breakout. Not only that, but unhealthy food can be inflammatory, and that will show up on the skin. A fresh, whole food, plant-based diet reduces hormone overexposure, and it can also reduce inflammation, leaving your skin smooth, calm, and blemish-free.

Reduced risk of disease: Heart disease, cancer, diabetes, and strokes will prematurely kill most of us who live in developed countries. The good news is that for every disease, from heart disease to cancer to diabetes, higher fruit and vegetable consumption is associated with reduced risk. We know that heart disease and type 2 diabetes can be prevented, managed, and reversed with a whole food, plant-based diet. We also know that many cancers can be delayed, slowed, or prevented altogether the same way.

Increased mental clarity and stability: Many raw food enthusiasts say they feel mentally clearer and more stable as a result of their raw food diet. When hormones are balanced, nutrients are plentiful, and proper hydration is achieved, we're more likely to feel mentally clear.

Raw Plant Foods Are Good for the Planet and Animals

Plant foods leave a smaller environmental footprint. Here's just one eye-opening statistic: One head of beef cattle can be raised on two acres (8,094 square meters) over two years' time, yielding about 500 pounds (227 kg) of meat. Over two years, that same two acres (8,094 square meters) can grow 30,000 pounds (13,608 kg) of high-quality plant foods, such as kale and quinoa.

The one beef cattle would have also used 15,000 to 20,000 gallons (56.8 to 75.7 kl) of water, produced tons of greenhouse gases, used massive amounts of labor-intensive stored hay, and eaten many of the crops for which genetically-modified organisms (GMOs) are created.

In the United States alone, ten billion animals are kept and killed for food every year. Each of those animals was a conscious, aware, and sentient individual whose life mattered very much to them. A vegan lifestyle won't eliminate all suffering, but it can go a long way in reducing unnecessary misery.

A Word about Kids

You might be wondering: Is a raw foods diet good for kids? Kids love fresh, live food and as long as they're getting enough calories, a raw food diet can be nutritionally sound for children. Kids also love creating with raw foods. Involve them in your raw food endeavors. Let them make some dishes of their own. They will end up with something to eat, but there is also the entertainment value of having a good time. They'll learn how to measure, count, plan, be self-sufficient, to enjoy and love food, and maybe to be a little adventurous.

chapter

Common Questions, Answered

Anyone who follows a plant-based diet or vegan lifestyle is going to hear the protein question sooner or later. Usually sooner, someone will inquire in a most serious and worried tone, "But where do you get your protein?"

This chapter will help you answer that question, and the similar ones you're sure to get.

"But Where Do You Get Your Protein?"

One correct answer to the protein question is, "Almost everywhere." An equally right response is, "From plants!" The factually correct response would be, "I get all the essential amino acids I need from plants, and my body makes them into the many proteins that it most wants and needs."

People have many common but incorrect beliefs, and a great deal of misinformation, about protein, including that protein is hard to get, builds muscles, only occurs in a very few and special foods, and that more is better.

The truth is that protein is common and abundant, and an excess intake can strain the kidneys and the liver and cause illness. Excess protein also helps cancer grow and thrive.

Protein isn't one uniform thing. There are about two million types of protein in the human body, all composed of linked chains of amino acids. So we don't really even need protein: What we need are amino acids. Those are the building blocks with which we make the type of protein that is ideal for our human bodies. Some amino acids are non-essential. Our bodies can make them, so we don't have to worry about getting them from our diet. Essential amino acids are the ones we need to obtain through our diet, and there are twenty of them.

Where Do We Get Essential Amino Acids in Our Diet?

Essential amino acids—the ones we obtain from our diet—are made by plants. Because plants are nutrient producers and animals are nutrient consumers, there is nothing in animal protein that did not originate in plants. Many leafy green vegetables contain as much as 20 to 45 percent protein in the form of amino acids. Fruit contains 5 to 8 percent protein, just like human breast milk.

All of our protein needs can be met with amino acids from plant foods and without the harm and excess protein often found in animal products.

Where Do You Get Calcium?

Most of us have heard that cow's milk grows strong bones. Right? But is that really true? In countries where milk consumption is high, rates of osteoporosis are also high. In countries where milk consumption is low, rates of osteoporosis are also low. That's found everywhere in the world, not just in isolated cases or anomalies.

Calcium is an important mineral for bone health. It can be found in plant foods in abundance, and plant-based calcium is more able to be absorbed and used in the body. Calcium is plentiful in dark leafy greens, broccoli, beans, almonds, flaxseeds, sesame seeds, Brazil nuts, and parsley.

But calcium is only one nutrient of many that work together in synergy to create healthy bones and teeth. Vitamin K is also essential to bone health, as are vitamin D and the mineral magnesium. Vitamin K is found in abundance in leafy green vegetables, especially kale. Vitamin D can be gotten from as little as fifteen to twenty minutes a day of sunlight exposure. And magnesium is plentifully found in nuts, seeds, fruits, and vegetables.

Bone health is also connected to heart health, and calcium in places outside the bones or teeth can be quite harmful. Calcification occurs when calcium salt is deposited in and on tissue. It's the process by which bones are made. But it's also one way that cardiovascular disease can develop. Calcium can deposit in soft tissue, such as the lining of arteries, creating the plaques that cause heart disease, heart attack, and stroke. Calcification can also happen in the heart valves, making them less able to function, causing an enlarged heart, and eventually, heart failure.

Calcium supplements and calcium from cow's milk can cause calcification in soft tissue. By obtaining calcium from plant sources, we get an easily absorbed type of calcium, and we also get the other nutrients, such as vitamin K and magnesium, that help to ensure the calcium will stay in our bones where it belongs.

For healthy bones, replace that morning cup of milk with a green smoothie. Almond, other nut milks, flax milk, and other seed milks are also delicious, easy to make, and provide a great deal of nutrition, including calcium.

What about Vitamin B12?

Vitamin B12 is essential for the health of the brain and nervous system. It isn't made by plants. It's not made by animals, either. B12 is made by soil microbes in the intestines. When we didn't wash our food well, we ingested these bacteria and made our own B12. Now that we're so hygienic, it's possible to run low on this vital nutrient.

But B12 supplements are easy to get and inexpensive. A sublingual tablet, one that is dissolved under the tongue, every day or every few days can provide all the B12 anyone needs.

How Is a Raw Diet Part of a Healthy Life?

Food is just one part of a healthy life. We need so much more. We need each component because they all work together. The human body can survive for only about four minutes without air. We can survive as long as a week without water, a week or so without sleep, and up to two months or more without food. We also require regular movement to keep a healthy body, and friendship and connection with others to really thrive. A raw foods diet supports all of these other parts of a healthy life. Let's talk about each in turn.

Air: How much time do you spend outdoors? It can be easy to simply go from the house to the car to the office, without ever stopping to smell the air. We need fresh air all year round. Every cell in our body benefits from good oxygen levels. Our skin gets rosy and pink when we're fully oxygenated, and our lungs are much more able to fight off respiratory infections when they've been exposed to fresh, outdoor air. Even weight loss and getting a good night's sleep are easier when getting lots of fresh air.

Water: The human body is 60 to 70 percent water. The brain is 75 percent water. Every action and reaction in your body relies on water. It's a solvent and a transporter, it regulates temperature and pH, it balances electrolytes, and it lubricates your joints, skin, eyes, and mouth. If a person loses just 1 percent of the water in her body, she will get thirsty. When 5 percent is lost, muscle strength and endurance decline. A loss of 10 percent will cause blurred vision and cognitive deficit. And death results when water loss approaches 20 percent.

Raw fruits and vegetables have plentiful water and are very hydrating. The plant acts as a natural filter, too, making the water in fresh produce quite pure. In addition to eating lots of raw fruits and vegetables, make sure to drink a half ounce (15 ml) of water for every pound (0.45 kg) of your body weight every day. A 150-pound (68.1-kg) person would drink a minimum of 75 ounces (2.2 L) of water. That's just over a half gallon. It's a good practice to begin the day with 24 to 32 ounces (710 to 946 ml) of water. You can add a little lemon juice for flavor.

Sleep: Good health requires good sleep. Chronic sleep loss can cause health problems, such as weight gain, high blood pressure, and high cholesterol, and it can also impair the immune system. It's been implicated in everything from heart disease to cancer.

Getting seven to nine hours of deep, restful sleep will help keep the heart healthy, reduce inflammation and stress, improve memory, stabilize moods, and aid in weight loss. Individual sleep needs vary, but most people need about eight hours of deep, restorative sleep each night. Contrary to common belief, the need for sleep doesn't decline as we age. Only our ability to sleep is lessened.

Food: "You are what you eat." That old saying is very literally true. Food is the most physically intimate relationship any of us will ever have. The food we eat becomes part of us. It's what builds our cells and also what provides our energy. Everything we are is a result of what we have eaten. That's why it's so important to eat a fresh, whole, raw food diet.

The list of the benefits and harm of various foods is long. In general, a diet high in fresh fruits and vegetables, and one that eliminates animal products, will reduce the risk of heart disease, diabetes, stroke, metabolic syndrome, vision loss due to macular degeneration, and obesity.

Epigenetics is the study of how gene expression is affected by environment. Researchers are finding that even small changes in lifestyle, including diet, can produce significant changes in gene expression, which can have negative or positive impacts on our health. What we do today can also affect our unborn children and their children as well. So choose your food wisely. You really are what you eat.

Movement: We're meant to move. Many functions in your body depend on it. Your lymph system, for example, is totally dependent on movement for circulation. The lymph system removes toxins, so when we don't move enough, we're left stewing in our own wastes. When we don't move, our joints get stiff and our muscles get tight. Some studies say that physical inactivity causes as many premature deaths as smoking.

Walking is excellent exercise that most of us can do and requires no equipment. Rebounding, which is using a small trampoline for gentle bouncing, is gentle on the knees and really gets the lymph system moving. Swimming, gardening, playing a sport, bike riding, and any activity that gets a body moving is going to be good for overall health. Many of these activities are free or inexpensive.

Friendship: Studies show that friendship and interaction are crucial to human health. We're social, and we need others to have a truly vibrant life. Friendships and other loving relationships can ease stress, help us feel safe and supported, allow us to confidently explore our world, and celebrate the good times and withstand the bad ones.

How Can Raw Help Me Avoid Harm?

"Doctor, doctor, it hurts when I do this!"
"Then don't do that!"
—Smith & Dale, vaudeville duo

For health, raw foods add to the diet what is good and healthy and remove what is harmful. They also exclude what traditionally must be cooked and what is also generally unhealthy, such as animal products, wheat, soy, refined sugars, corn syrup, processed grains, and the various chemicals that are used to flavor and preserve processed foods. It's also wise to avoid excessive caffeine, too much alcohol, and cigarette smoke.

chapter

3

> **"** Tell me what you eat, and I will tell you who you are. **"**
>
> —Jean Anthelme Brillat-Savarin, French politician and gastronome

Choosing Raw Foods

"I'd love to eat healthy, but it's *so* expensive!"

If I had a nickel for every time I heard that, I'd be rich. But is it true? To be honest, it *can* be true. A raw food diet is often portrayed as requiring lots of expensive and obscure superfoods and exotic ingredients. Those kinds of products are usually quite expensive and can even take a healthy diet out of the realm of possibility for many people.

I rarely use exotic superfoods and have not used any in this book. I stick to the produce department in my local grocery. For example, kale is the best and most powerful superfood available, and it can be found in most groceries at affordable prices.

Any recipe or dish is only as good as its ingredients. In this chapter, we'll discuss how to buy the freshest produce possible without breaking the bank and how to protect your investment by storing it properly before using it to guarantee the best possible results and nutritional benefits.

Buying Raw Foods on a Budget

Buying high-quality, fresh, organic produce in large quantities can get expensive. But there are ways to keep the costs reasonable. Here are some of the most effective.

Buy in bulk. Buying in bulk is one of the bargain shopper's best strategies. Larger warehouse-type stores can have lower prices. When stores are running a good sale, stock up and preserve any extras by freezing or drying. Often, the owner or manager of a grocery store will allow shoppers to buy fruits and vegetables by the case, which can reduce the cost per item. But you have to ask. Ask to see your produce manager and get to know him or her. He or she can also give you tips on buying and storing what is available and will often let you know of upcoming sales and bulk purchase opportunities.

Buy in season. When things are plentiful, they're less expensive. In the summer, when produce is at its peak, there can be incredible sales on produce such as tomatoes, peppers, corn, and berries. As the season turns to fall, apples and raspberries will be plentiful and less expensive than they are at other times during the year. Prices for produce from non-local sources will also wax and wane with availability. Eat what is most abundantly available and store the rest.

Shop at farmers' markets. Farmers' markets often offer the freshest and least-expensive produce around. If there's one nearby, you will save a few dollars and have the opportunity to establish a connection with the people who grow your food. Heirlooms and unusual varieties of fruits and vegetables are also often sold at farmers' markets. It can be money saving and an adventure at the same time.

Join a CSA. CSA stands for community supported agriculture. Generally, the way it works is that the grower sells shares of his future harvest. The members of the CSA then share the harvest. Usually, each member will receive a box of fresh produce each week. It's an excellent way to form a relationship with your grower and others in your community, but there might be times when you need to supplement your weekly box with grocery store or farmers' market produce.

Be selective about organic produce. It's true: Organic produce is usually more expensive that nonorganic. And, in most cases, organic produce is best. Organic fruits and vegetables are grown with natural fertilizers and pesticides, which are usually less toxic than those used in conventional farming. Organic is often better for your health and can produce less pollution when grown. But if you're trying to keep costs down and still make sure you have plenty of healthy, fresh food available, cut back on the organics, or at least some organics. Some produce has a much lower chance of having pesticide and herbicide residue than others.

Here are some foods that appear regularly on the Environmental Working Group's "Dirty Dozen" list and are best to buy organic: apples, celery, strawberries, peaches, spinach, nectarines, grapes, bell peppers, blueberries, lettuce, and kale.

Here are some foods that appear regularly on the Environmental Working Group's "Clean 15" list and can be bought conventionally grown: onions, corn, pineapples, avocado, asparagus, peas, mangoes, cantaloupe, kiwifruit, cabbage, watermelon, sweet potatoes, grapefruit, and mushrooms.

Grow your own. This might be the best money-saving tip of all. For the price of seeds, seedlings, and a little bit of ef-

At the Grocery Store

Here are some tips to keep to your budget when you're planning meals and buying groceries.

- Buy in season, and purchase local items when possible. Prices will be lowest on the most bountiful produce, so things that are in season will often carry the smallest price tag.

- Get to know your grocery store owner or manager. He or she who will know all the best deals and when the freshest items are available.

- Get to know the schedule of when the produce department puts out new, fresh items. Shopping when things are fresh will save money by reducing the chance of spoilage.

- When things go on sale, stock up. Freeze or dehydrate the surplus for later use.

- Buy cases of frequently used items. Often, the price per case will be significantly less expensive than buying one item at a time.

- When not eating raw, cooked rice, lentils, quinoa, sweet potatoes, and squash are excellent, healthy, and economical foods.

- Put love and intention into food. It's free, but oh-so-valuable.

fort, you can grow a good-size garden. Or, if not a garden, at least you could grow a windowsill full of greens, herbs, and sprouts. Growing your own will ensure the highest quality. Outside, tomatoes, peppers, beans, lettuces, and kale are easy to grow and are good performers. Inside, sprouts of all kinds do well in jars, and baby greens, sunflower seed sprouts (see how-to page 40), and herbs will flourish.

Preserving the Bounty

Buying in bulk can save money and time, but it also can result in spoiled and wasted food if you don't plan ahead and store food properly. Here are some ways to preserve the surplus and enjoy it later in the year.

On the kitchen counter: Bananas, apples, avocados, peaches, pears, and many other fruits and some vegetables can be stored at room temperature on the kitchen counter for up to a few days. If not perfectly ripe, leave fruits on the counter until they are and then either move them into the refrigerator, or freeze them for up to several months.

Refrigerating: Most produce will stay fresh in the refrigerator for a week or longer. It's true that some nutrients are lost in storage, but refrigeration will slow down that process, and freezing nearly brings it to a halt. Fruits will keep better in a lidded container, but they shouldn't be washed before storing. Lettuce and greens can be washed, dried, and stored wrapped in paper towels in a lidded container. They will store best if given some air circulation, but not so much that they dry out or wilt.

A badly functioning refrigerator can cause foods to stay too warm or even to freeze. Food that's not kept cold enough will spoil. Freezing won't change the nutritional content of food, but will leave it in poor shape for some uses. So get a thermometer, check your refrigerator, and make sure it's cooling properly. Most of the fruits and vegetables in this book will do best when refrigerated at 32 to 34°F (0 to 1°C) and 95 percent humidity.

Store fruit separately from vegetables. Fruit releases ethylene gas that can shorten the storage life of vegetables.

Here's one exception to the rule of produce staying fresher in the fridge: bananas. Their skins turn brown when exposed to cold, including refrigeration. Store bananas on the counter until they're perfectly ripe, then move any that can't be used right away straight into the freezer.

How to Tell When Produce Is Perfectly Ripe

Smell is perhaps the best indicator when most fruits have reached their peak. A ripe fruit will smell good and have a fairly strong aroma. Here are some specifics.

- Pears, peaches, nectarines, plums, and mangoes are ripe when they have a pleasant aroma and are just slightly soft.

- Bananas are ripe when the skins turn golden yellow and develop brown flecks.

- Pineapple should remain firm and not mushy. It will have a pleasant pineapple aroma, and the leaves on the top will be easy to pull off.

- Cantaloupes will be heavy for their size, and the stem end will smell deliciously of cantaloupe.

- Watermelon will not ripen any further once it has been picked, but a large yellow spot on the bottom will mean it's ripe.

- Apples will be firm, with no blemishes.

- Berries will be fully colored and plump.

And how about vegetables? Most vegetables, such as squash or lettuces, can be used at any stage from immature to ripe.

Freezing: You might be wondering: Are frozen foods still raw? The short answer is, yes. If a food has not been previously heated and is frozen, then it's still raw when it's later thawed and used. As an added benefit, it hasn't spent days on the shelf or in the refrigerator losing nutrients.

Freezing fruits and vegetables when they're in season and at the peak of their freshness can also save you money compared with buying them out of season. Be aware when buying frozen foods, though, because commercial frozen vegetables will often have been blanched (briefly boiled) before freezing. Fruits and berries are usually left raw.

What frozen foods cannot do is thaw out and return to their previous unfrozen state. Water expands when it freezes, bursting the cell walls within the fruit or vegetable. This doesn't reduce the nutrition in the food significantly, but many thawed foods will be soft, flabby, or watery. So frozen foods are ideal for smoothies, soups, and sauces, but they will be too soft and flabby to eat fresh or in salads. Nuts, avocados, and any high-fat or dry food, will have little water to expand and can retain their condition very well.

To freeze your own fruits and vegetables, simply clean the fruit or vegetable and dry it well. Cut large fruits and vegetables into smaller pieces, and leave smaller items, such as berries, whole. To prevent food from sticking together once frozen, spread the items in a single layer on a cookie sheet and freeze through. Once frozen, transfer them into lidded containers, if possible, or in freezer boxes or bags. There's no need to blanch any item before freezing.

As mentioned before, one fruit that freezes well is avocados. Just cut them in half, put them wrapped in a lidded container or in a freezer bag, and freeze. Allow at least a couple hours for them to thaw, and they'll be perfect for use in dressings, puddings, and smoothies.

Drying: Some foods can be stored well after they've been dried. Tomatoes, most fruits and berries, hot peppers, red peppers, and most herbs can be easily stored once they've been dried in a dehydrator until nearly all their moisture has been removed. It's important that all moisture is gone to ensure the food can be stored long term. Most things will be dry in 24 hours or less if dehydrated at 118°F (48°C). Once dried, store in a lidded container at room temperature for several weeks, or in the freezer for up to several months.

Avoid Plastics

Plastics are in our cars, cans, computers, phones, toys, containers, packaging, composite dental fillings, and nearly everything we use every day. They're truly ubiquitous and impossible to avoid. But it's a good idea to avoid plastic containers for food when we can.

Virtually all plastic contains endocrine disruptors, such as (but not limited to) bisphenyl-A (BPA), which was originally manufactured as a synthetic estrogen. It was soon discovered that BPA worked even better as an additive to plastics, making them tough and durable. But we're learning that what's good for plastics is bad for the human body. Endocrine disruptors can affect the immune system, cause weight gain and infertility, initiate premature puberty, and worsen PMS and perimenopause symptoms.

Temperature also makes a difference. Heat causes more toxins to leach out of plastic containers and into the food they hold. Food that is frozen and then placed in a plastic freezer bag will cause little leaching. Warm or hot food will cause more.

It would be difficult, and perhaps impossible, to entirely avoid plastic. Sometimes, it's simply a great deal more convenient to use plastic. Alternatives, depending on what needs to be stored, are glass, stainless steel, paper, and cloth. Many items can be stored in the refrigerator or freezer in lidded glass or stainless steel containers or jars. Other items will do well wrapped in paper or cloth. Paper or cloth bags work well for both transport and storage.

4

> "Do not wait; the time will never be 'just right.' Start where you stand, and work with whatever tools you may have at your command, and better tools will be found as you go along."
>
> —*Napoleon Hill, author* Think and Grow Rich

Tools & Techniques

As you get started, you'll need to gather a few essential tools and master some basic techniques to get your raw lifestyle up and running. These processes will become quick and easy, and they will save you a lot of money in the long run, versus buying their premade counterparts!

Spending just a little time and money outfitting and organizing your raw food kitchen will pay off big in ease and convenience.

Creating a new lifestyle, to a great extent, is a process of creating new habits. Any new venture begins with some confusion and uncertainty. At first, it can be difficult to organize the week and even the day. But how exciting! Change can be invigorating. You'll use many of these techniques on a regular basis, and they can become new habits that are second nature. Making nut milks, for example, is something that many of us will do almost daily. Use these techniques to get started, and then adapt them to your own needs and schedule.

Essential Equipment

Raw food doesn't have to be complicated. A few apples or bananas in hand could be a small raw food meal that requires no tools at all. A blender and food processor are needed for many of the recipes in this book. But don't let a lack of expensive equipment stop you from beginning a raw food diet or lifestyle. Just use what you have, and acquire new tools as you can.

Knives: Good knives can really come in handy in a raw food kitchen, and they should be considered essential. High-carbon stainless steel is an excellent material. It keeps a sharp edge, won't stain or rust, and is of better quality than ordinary stainless steel. Ceramic knives are also desirable. They're very hard, keep a sharp edge, don't impart a flavor to food, and are lightweight.

One or two well-made knives will be a better bargain than many lesser-quality tools. A 5- to 6-inch (13 to 15 cm) utility knife and a 7- to 8-inch (17 to 20 cm) chef's knife will be versatile and do most of the work in any raw kitchen. They are both perfect for chopping, mincing, and slicing. A serrated knife can come in handy for slicing skinned fruits such as tomatoes, and a cleaver works very well for chopping herbs.

When buying knives, it's best to see how the knife feels in your hand. Try it on for size before buying. The knife should sit well in your hand, and the grip should be comfortable.

Lightweight knives are good for speedy and precise chopping and slicing of fruits and vegetables. A heavier knife is ideal for chopping harder materials, such as nuts, fresh ginger, and blocks of cacao paste. Two or three good-quality knives in common sizes and weights should be plenty to get you started.

Blender: Once the kitchen is outfitted with suitable knives, a blender is next on the essentials list. A good blender is a powerhouse that will do things that can't be done by hand and will make quick work of pureeing soups and smoothies, grinding nuts and seeds, and crushing ice.

More speeds are not necessarily better. Three speeds with a pulse option is a good place to start. A large jar or carafe, at least 40 ounces (1.2 L), will offer flexibility for soups and smoothies and other large-batch items. A smaller, bullet-type blender will be helpful for smaller-batch items, such as nut cheeses, condiments, and salad dressings. Keep in mind that more expensive blenders will have better performance in most instances, but the lower priced machines will get the job done, too.

Food processor: A food processor with an "S" blade is almost as handy as a blender, and it's especially suited for processing large quantities. It will chop, mince, slice, puree, and shred. It can be used to make pie fillings, cookie dough, nut butters, and salsas. It's essential for making nut and date pie crusts.

Look for a food processor with a medium- to large-size bowl, anywhere from 6 to 9 cups (1.4 to 2.13 L) or more. Some processors will come with a detachable 2- to 4-cup (470 to 940 ml) mini bowl. This is optional, but it can be useful for smaller amounts.

If you don't have a food processor, a blender can be used for many processing jobs instead.

Spice/coffee grinder: A spice or coffee grinder is a small appliance that will grind small amounts of nuts, seeds,

herbs, and more. It's not absolutely essential, but it can make most raw food recipes go smoothly. Clean it with a stiff bristled brush or a damp cloth.

If you don't have a spice grinder, a small blender can be used to grind dried herbs and spices instead.

Dehydrator: A dehydrator can make a raw food life easier and convenient. This machine will ideally have a temperature setting that can be adjusted to 118°F (48°C) or below, as well as a fan that will blow air over the food that's drying.

If you don't have a dehydrator, a warm oven, set at the lowest temperature with the door slightly ajar, can be easily substituted for a dehydrator.

Nut milk bags: Nut milk bags are used to strain the pulp from nut and seed milks. You can purchase them online. Natural fiber bags are best and will be the most long lasting and durable. Hemp bags are particularly sturdy. Nylon bags are also available, but have a tendency to wear out quickly. Bags made with hemp fiber are particularly durable and work very well.

If you don't have a nut milk bag, several layers of cheesecloth can be used to strain milks instead.

Spirooli/spiralizer: A spirooli or spiralizer will make quick work of turning nearly any vegetable, and even a few fruits, into long, delectable noodles. Zucchini, beets, carrots, apples, and even pears will easily fit into the machine, and with a few easy turns of the handle, produce mounds of veggie "pasta." Purchase this handy tool online.

If you don't have a spirooli, use a knife and vegetable peeler to make noodles. (See instructions on page 43.)

Juicer: A juicer is not necessary for the majority of the recipes in this book. However, a good juicer can be of great value in a raw kitchen. Two types of juicers are centrifugal and masticating. Centrifugal juicers are the most common, and they work best for citrus, other fruits, and vegetables. A masticating juicer will work well with wheat grass.

If you don't have a juicer, puree fruits and vegetables in a blender until as smooth as possible and then strain the liquid through a nut milk bag.

Salad spinner: Dry salads and vegetables hold their dressings much better than wet ones do. A salad spinner is the perfect gadget to get your greens as dry as possible. Centrifugal force pushes water away from the salad fixings. Salad spinners are handy to have, though not essential, and they can be found in most department, kitchen, and home supply stores for reasonable prices.

If you don't have a salad spinner, drain greens in a colander and pat dry with a towel.

Ice cream maker: Banana ice cream requires only a food processor. But if you'd like to make other ice creams more than a few times a year, you will probably want to consider purchasing an ice cream maker. Electric machines with a frozen canister are good midrange choices, and they will be the most versatile.

If you don't have an ice cream maker, just place any ice cream in the freezer and stir every half hour until it has firmed.

Storage containers: Glass is usually the best material for a storage container, although sometimes plastic can be easier to use and more convenient. (See "Avoid Plastics" on page 24.) Canning jars with lids, lidded glass bowls, and plastic boxes and bags are some of the options that are good to have on hand in which to store raw food supplies and leftovers.

Other gadgets: A garlic press, large and small grater, vegetable peeler, micro plane, and citrus press aren't essential, but they can make time in the kitchen easier and more convenient. Plus, they're fun. Collect these, and other kitchen tools, as you go and as you can afford them. Raw food is, ideally, simple and easy to prepare.

Techniques

Raw food isn't cooked with heat, but still there are techniques and skills that can make a raw food life easier and more convenient and the dishes tastier and even more appealing. Some of the techniques include produce preparation, dehydrating, soaking and drying nuts, soaking and sprouting grains and legumes, drying fruit, and preserving produce and herbs.

Soaking, Drying, and Storing Nuts and Seeds

Nuts and seeds are nature's perfectly designed packages. They're full of nutrition, and they're essential in any raw kitchen. But you can't use just any nuts.

Most commercially available nuts have been roasted. Look for nuts that are labeled as raw. Many nuts will not be fully raw because some, such as cashews and almonds, for example, are often heated during processing. Even so, roasting happens at a much higher temperature, and those labeled raw will have been minimally heated.

Nuts and seeds hold the potential for new life, and they must be able to withstand a hostile environment until there is a suitable opportunity to grow. They regulate their germination with enzyme inhibitors. Water is the key to life, and soaking conveys the message to nuts and seeds that growing conditions are good. The enzyme inhibitors are washed

How to Open an Avocado

Slice avocado lengthwise down center, rotating knife around pit, and cutting through to seed all the way around. Twist two halves apart. Use a knife and hit blade into the avocado pit and twist to remove pit. Slice avocado and scoop from the peel.

away, and the seed begins to change. Because of this, most nuts will benefit from soaking before using.

Many nuts, especially those with brown skins such as hazelnuts, walnuts, and pecans, are high in tannins. Tannins protect plants from insects and bacteria and help regulate growth, but they can also be bitter, hard to digest, and astringent. Soaking will remove much of the tannins.

The soaking water will turn brown quite quickly as the tannins are washed away, and the water should be changed if it gets too brown.

Soaking and drying nuts can also make them more flavorful and easier to digest.

Soaking nuts and seeds: To soak nuts or seeds, place them in a glass bowl with enough water to cover them by a few inches. (A glass container is recommended for soaking because of the chemicals that may leach into the food with prolonged contact with plastics.) Make sure to use enough water to account for how much the nuts and seeds will absorb. Then, to every 4 cups (940 ml) of water used for soaking, add 1 tablespoon (18 g) of salt. This will help further eliminate the enzyme inhibitors. Replace the water after an hour or so if it has turned very brown.

Allow the nuts or seeds to soak for about eight hours or overnight. Then drain and rinse them well.

Some recipes, such as those for nut milks, require nuts that have been soaked and not dried. So if you are soaking, but not drying the nuts, store them in a covered container in the refrigerator for up to three days or in the freezer for up to several months.

Drying nuts and seeds: To dry nuts and seeds, spread them out in a single, even layer on an unlined dehydrator sheet. Dehydrate them at 118°F (48°C) for twenty-four hours or until they are absolutely dry without any moisture at all. They should feel very dry to the touch with no detectable moisture.

Storing nuts and seeds: Nuts and seeds contain lots of healthy but delicate fats. Many will go rancid after a short while at room temperature. Nuts and seeds can be stored in a tightly lidded container at room temperature for about a week, or in the freezer for up to several months. Nuts and seeds can be stored in the freezer before or after they've been soaked and dried.

How to Cut and Section a Grapefruit

Using a sharp knife, slice top and bottom ends off. This will help it sit flat on cutting board. Then slice off remaining peel, cutting from top to bottom and following the fruit's curve. Cut each section just inside membrane and remove flesh.

Making Nut and Seed Milk

Nut and seed milks are nutritious, delicious, and easy to make. They provide healthy fats. They can be enjoyed on their own, used over raw cereals, or added to smoothies.Here are the basic instructions to make any nut or seed milk. You can use any combination of nuts and seeds.

1. Rinse and soak the nuts or seeds overnight in a glass bowl with enough water to cover them by a few inches.

2. Drain and rinse the nuts or seeds well.

3. In a blender, puree the nuts or seeds and water—using a ratio of nuts and seeds to water of 1 : 3 to 1 : 4—until smooth. This may take several minutes, depending on the strength of your blender. For thicker, cream-like milk, use a nut-to-water ratio of 1 : 2.

4. This unstrained milk can be used just as it is, without straining. It will still contain all the fiber and other nutrients found in the pulp.

5. If a smoother drink is desired, strain the milk through a nut milk bag or a few layers of cheesecloth into a bowl or large-mouthed jar. Squeeze the pulp in the nut milk bag or the cheesecloth until as much liquid as possible has been removed.

6. Add a pinch of salt if desired and stir.

7. For sweetened milk, add 1 to 2 tablespoons (15 to 28 ml) of agave, a dropper or two of stevia, or date paste, coconut palm crystals, or maple syrup to taste.

8. If desired, add optional flavorings, such as cinnamon, ginger, nutmeg, cardamom, vanilla, or even cayenne.

9. Store the milk in a tightly lidded glass jar for up to three days in the refrigerator or up to several months in the freezer. Shake the container well before serving.

10. Use the milk in recipes, or add it to smoothies for a nutritional boost.

Simple Unsweetened Almond Milk

This is the most basic almond milk, and it's a good all-purpose, unsweetened milk for use in most recipes.

1 cup (145 g) almonds, soaked overnight, rinsed well, and drained

5 cups (1.2 L) water

Pinch of salt

Place all of the ingredients in a blender, puree until smooth, and then strain through a nut milk bag, squeezing to get as much of the milk out as possible.

Store the milk in a glass jar or other container in the refrigerator for up to 3 days.

YIELD: ABOUT 4½ CUPS (1 L)

Simple Sweetened Almond Milk

A sweeter almond milk is just as easy to make as the unsweetened and is also a staple in any raw food kitchen. It goes well with raw cereals and can be used in smoothies or any recipe calling for sweetened nut milk.

1 cup (145 g) almonds, soaked overnight, rinsed well, and drained

5 cups (1.2 L) water

2 to 3 tablespoons (30 to 45 ml) agave or maple syrup

1 teaspoon vanilla extract or vanilla powder

⅛ teaspoon salt

Place the nuts and water in a blender and puree until very smooth. Strain through a nut milk bag, squeezing to get as much of the milk out as possible.

Add the agave or maple syrup, vanilla, and salt to the finished milk and stir well.

Store the milk in a glass jar or other container in the refrigerator for up to 3 days.

YIELD: ABOUT 5½ CUPS (1.3 L)

Sweet Hazelnut and Sunflower Seed Milk

This sweet and flavorful milk cuts costs by using less-expensive sunflower seeds in addition to the more pricey hazelnuts. A little agave sweetens the milk nicely.

- 1 **cup (135 g) hazelnuts, soaked overnight**
- ½ **cup (65 g) shelled sunflower seeds, soaked overnight**
- 6 **cups (1.4 L) water**
- 2 **tablespoons (30 ml) agave**
- 1 **teaspoon vanilla extract**
  Pinch of salt

Place all of the ingredients in a blender, puree until smooth, and then strain through a nut milk bag, squeezing to get as much of the milk out as possible.

Store the milk in a glass jar or other container in the refrigerator for up to 3 days.

YIELD: ABOUT 5½ CUPS (1.3 L)

Brazil Nut and Walnut Milk

The combination of nuts and seeds in the recipe gives it a creamy and complex feel and flavor. A little added cinnamon can warm it up and adds an additional layer of flavor.

- ½ **cup (75 g) Brazil nuts, soaked overnight**
- ½ **cup (50 g) walnuts, soaked overnight**
- ½ **cup (65 g) shelled sunflower seeds, soaked overnight**
- 6 **cups (1.4 L) water**
  Pinch of salt
- 2 to 3 **tablespoons (30 to 45 ml) agave**
- 1 **teaspoon vanilla extract or vanilla powder**
- 1 **teaspoon ground cinnamon (optional)**

Place the nuts and water in a blender and puree until very smooth. Strain through a nut milk bag, squeezing to get as much of the milk out as possible.

To the finished milk, add the agave.

Store the milk in a glass jar or other container in the refrigerator for up to 3 days.

YIELD: ABOUT 6¾ CUPS (1.5 L)

Sweet and Creamy Cashew and Macadamia Nut Milk

Cashews and macadamias combine here to make what is possibly the creamiest and most delicious milk ever. Use maple syrup or agave to sweeten.

- 1 cup (145 g) cashews, soaked overnight
- ½ cup (70 g) macadamia nuts, soaked overnight
- 5 cups (1.2 L) water
- 3 tablespoons (45 ml) maple syrup or agave
  Pinch of salt

Place all of the ingredients in a blender and puree until smooth and then strain through a nut milk bag, squeezing to get as much of the milk out as possible.

Store the milk in a glass jar or other container in the refrigerator for up to 3 days.

YIELD: ABOUT 5½ CUPS (1.2 L)

Almond and Flaxseed Milk

Flaxseeds add a good dose of healthy omega-3 fats to this delicious and healthy milk which also contains a wide variety of the different forms of vitamin E.

- 1 cup (145 g) almonds, soaked overnight
- ½ cup (50 g) finely ground flaxseeds
- 6 cups (1.4 L) water
- 2 tablespoons (30 ml) agave
  Pinch of salt
- ½ teaspoon ground cinnamon (optional)
- ½ teaspoon ground cardamom (optional)

Place all of the ingredients in a blender, puree until smooth, and then strain through a nut milk bag, squeezing to get as much of the milk out as possible.
Store the milk in a glass jar or other container in the refrigerator for up to 3 days.

YIELD: ABOUT 6½ CUPS (1.5 L)

Chocolate Milk

Sweet and chocolaty, this is a simple and quick chocolate milk that's delicious and downright decadent. But this is no guilty pleasure. The almond milk is high in calcium, and the cacao is chock full of antioxidants.

- 2 cups (470 ml) unsweetened almond milk or flax milk
- 2 tablespoons (10 g) cacao powder
- 2 tablespoons (30 ml) agave
- 1 or 2 droppers stevia (or to taste)

Place all of the ingredients in a blender and puree until smooth.

YIELD: 2¼ CUPS (759 ML)

Unsweetened and Sweetened Vanilla Flax Milk

Flax milk may just be the tastiest, healthiest, and least expensive milk of all. It's also very simple to make, requires minimal soaking, and comes together in just minutes. The best part is that a quart of flax milk can be made for mere pennies.

¼ cup (42 g) flaxseeds, finely ground
4 cups (940 ml) water
½ teaspoon salt
2 tablespoons (30 ml) agave (optional)
1 teaspoon vanilla extract (optional)

Place the flaxseeds and water in a blender and let them soak for about 15 minutes. Then blend on high speed until the seeds are fully broken down and the liquid looks like milk. Strain through a nut milk bag or a few layers of cheesecloth into a bowl or large-mouthed jar. Squeeze well to make sure no milk is wasted. Then add the salt and stir. For sweetened vanilla-flavored milk, add the agave and vanilla extract and stir well.

YIELD: 3¼ CUPS (759 ML)

Strawberry Milk

This milk is much like the colored, flavored, and sweetened milks kids enjoy, but this version is all natural and chemical free.

2 cups (470 ml) unsweetened almond milk
  or flax milk
½ cup (80 g) sliced strawberries
2 tablespoons (30 ml) agave (optional)
1 dropper stevia (or to taste)

Place all of the ingredients in a blender and puree until smooth.

YIELD: 2½ CUPS (590 ML)

Making Nut Butter

Store-bought nut butters can often be expensive, especially those that are raw. That's why it's so great that making your own nut butters is easy. All you need are nuts, a food processor, and patience—lots of patience.

Here are the basic instructions to make nut butter. You can use any nut or seed alone or in combination, including almonds, cashews, Brazil nuts, macadamia nuts, pecans, pistachios, hazelnuts, walnuts, sunflower seeds, pumpkin seeds, and flaxseeds.

1. To make 1 pound (455 g) of nut butter, use approximately 1 pound (455 g) of nuts, soaked and dehydrated, and ½ teaspoon salt.

2. Place the nuts and salt in a food processor fitted with an "S" blade. Process the nuts until they turn into nut butter. That sounds like a much faster process than it actually is. It will take as long as 15 to 20 minutes to process nuts into nut butter, so patience really is needed for this project.

3. Scrape down the sides as needed. The machine will also heat up the nut butter and may need to be stopped every so often to allow it to cool down.

4. Add agave, maple syrup, dates, or other sweeteners, if desired.

Maple Cinnamon Almond Butter

This is sweet, and the cinnamon adds an interesting layer of flavor. The flavor combination really reminds me of fall.

- 1 **pound (455 g) almonds, soaked and dried**
- ¼ **cup (60 ml) maple syrup**
- 3 **tablespoons (45 ml) olive oil**
- 1 **teaspoon ground cinnamon**
- ½ **teaspoon salt**

Place the almonds in a food processor and process for several minutes to ½ hour until they turn into nut butter. Gently stir in the remaining ingredients until well incorporated. Store in a glass jar in the refrigerator for up to several weeks.

YIELD: ABOUT 1 POUND (455 G)

Cacao Cashew Butter

Cashews make this a delightfully creamy, chocolaty concoction that's perfect on crackers or breads or in smoothies.

- 1 **pound (455 g) cashews, soaked and dried**
- 2 **tablespoons (30 ml) agave**
- 2 **tablespoons (30 ml) maple syrup**
- ½ **cup (40 g) cacao powder**
- ¼ **cup (60 ml) olive oil**
- 1 **teaspoon vanilla extract**

Place the soaked and dried cashews in a food processor and process for several minutes until they turn into nut butter. Gently stir in the remaining ingredients until well incorporated. Store in a glass jar in the refrigerator for up to several weeks.

YIELD: ABOUT 1 POUND (455 G)

Five Nut and Seed Butter with Omega-3

The five different nuts and seeds make this butter complex as well as more economical.

- ½ cup (75 g) almonds, soaked and dried
- ½ cup (75 g) cashews, soaked and dried
- ½ cup (50 g) walnuts, soaked and dried
- ½ cup (65 g) shelled sunflower seeds, soaked and dried
- ½ cup (50 g) ground flaxseeds
- ½ teaspoon salt

Place all of the ingredients in a food processor and process for several minutes until they turn into nut butter.

YIELD: ABOUT 2 CUPS (520 G)

Pumpkin Pie Nut and Seed Butter

Perfect for fall, this butter is spicy and sweet. It reminds me of a pumpkin pie.

- 1 cup (145 g) cashews, soaked and dried
- ¼ cup (35 g) almonds, soaked and dried
- ½ cup (50 g) ground flaxseeds
- ½ cup (65 g) shelled sunflower seeds, soaked and dried
- ¼ cup (60 ml) maple syrup or agave
- 1 teaspoon ground cinnamon
- ½ teaspoon ground nutmeg
- ½ teaspoon ground ginger
- ¼ teaspoon ground allspice
- ½ teaspoon salt

Place the nuts and seeds in a food processor and process for several minutes until they turn into nut butter. Gently stir in the remaining ingredients until well incorporated. Store in a glass jar in the refrigerator for up to several weeks.

YIELD: ABOUT 2¹/₂ CUPS (520 G)

Soaking and Drying Buckwheat Groats

Buckwheat groats are hard and dense seeds. But they become delightfully light, crispy, and easy to chew when soaked and dried. Here are simple steps to soaking them.

1. First rinse them very well using a metal mesh strainer. Buckwheat has a gelatinous coating when wet, and this needs to be rinsed away. Just spray water through them until the gel is gone.

2. Once they are well rinsed, place the buckwheat groats in a glass bowl or other container.

3. Cover them with water, making sure the water is 1 to 2 inches (2.5 to 5 cm) above the groats, because they will absorb quite a bit of liquid.

4. Place the container in the refrigerator and allow the buckwheat to soak for about 24 hours.

5. Drain the water from the groats.

6. Rinse the groats well once again using the strainer.

7. Spread them out in a single layer on lined dehydrator sheets. Dehydrate at 118°F (48°C) for several hours or overnight until all the moisture is gone. Stir the buckwheat occasionally to ensure even drying. Make sure all moisture is gone to prevent mold fromgrowing in the stored groats.

8. Store the dried buckwheat groats in a sealed jar or container at room temperature for up to a month. Or store them in the freezer for up to several months.

Growing Sunflower
Seed Sprouts

Sunflower seed sprouts can be tasty, super nutritious, and economical, too. Once you have a few pieces of necessary equipment, they're easy to grow. They will provide fresh greens year round.

You will need a growing tray of some kind and some soilless potting mix. A growing tray with drainage holes in the bottom will work best and prevent overwatering. Place the tray on another plastic lined tray to catch any water overflow. You will also need raw sunflower seeds with the shell still intact. Black oil sunflower seeds work really well for sprouting.

Cover the entire tray with a sheet of wet newspaper. The newspaper will hold in the moisture while the seeds are germinating. Place in a warm, dark area and check for germination. Remove the newspaper as soon as the seeds begin to sprout, which should only take a day or two.

Once the seeds have begun to sprout, move the tray to a sunny window. Water the sprouts gently once or twice a day when the soil begins to dry out, and keep the soil uniformly moist but not soggy.

Soak 1 cup (140 g) of sunflower seeds in water for 24 to 48 hours. Then rinse and drain them well. Place the soaked and drained seeds in a glass or ceramic bowl and cover with a damp cloth. The sunflower seed shells will split, and the seeds will sprout and develop a small tail-like root within a day or two. Once about half of them have the beginnings of a root, they are ready to plant.

Put ½ inch (1.3 cm) of soilless potting mix in the bottom of the growing tray. Spread the soaked sunflower seeds on the potting mix in a single layer, making sure they are evenly spaced and not overlapping. Cover the seeds with ⅛ inch (3 mm) potting mix. Gently water the soil until it's uniformly damp, but not soaking.

The sprouts are ready to harvest when they have two well-developed leaves and another pair of leaves is just starting to form. They will be about 3 to 4 inches (7.5 to 10 cm) tall. Depending on the growing conditions, it will take a week or two for the sprouts to reach harvest size.

Cut the sunflower sprout stems at their base and use them in salads, wraps, and smoothies.

Sunflower sprouts can be stored wrapped or in an airtight container in the refrigerator for up to a week

Buckwheat sprouts and wheat grass can be easily grown using this method as well. Simply substitute buckwheat groats or wheat berries for the sunflower seeds, and grow in the same manner. Harvest the buckwheat sprouts for salads and the wheat grass for juicing when they're about 3 inches (7.5 cm) tall.

Sprouting Lentils

To sprout lentils means to soak them, then keep them moist long enough for them to germinate and begin to grow a small root. It takes about 48 hours from start to finish. Sprouting lentils will increase the availability of nutrients and make them softer and more digestible. You'll need 1 cup (192 g) lentils and 2 cups (470 ml) water.

1. Place the lentils in a glass bowl and cover them with the water.

2. Soak the lentils in the water for about 8 hours or overnight.

3. Drain and rinse them well and place them in a bowl.

4. Cover the bowl with a wet paper towel and set in a warm, dark place.

5. Check the lentils and rinse them twice a day to keep moist.

6. Store them in a lidded container in the refrigerator for up to a week.

Making Vegetable "Pasta"

Using a spirooli, vegetable spiralizer, or a knife and vegetable peeler, you can turn fruits and vegetables such as zucchini, cucumbers, and beets into lovely "noodles" and "pastas" that can be served with a variety of sauces.

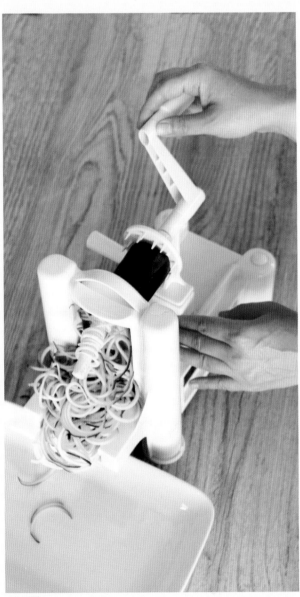

To make vegetable "pasta" using a spirooli or vegetable spiralizer, simply insert each end of the vegetable in the machine and turn the handle.

Then use a vegetable peeler to shave off thin or thick "noodles."

Drying Mangoes and Cherries

Dried cherries and dried mangoes are sweet, tart, chewy treats that can be used in cereals, granolas, truffles, and energy bars, and on top of ice creams, and more. They're easy and economical to make at home. Plus, when you make them, they won't have any of the chemicals that are commonly found in store-bought dried fruits.

To dry cherries, wash them and dry them well. Pit the cherries using a knife or cherry pitter. Then spread them in a single layer on a lined dehydrator sheet. Dehydrate at 118°F (48°C) for several hours or overnight. When the cherries are almost dry, flip them to ensure they are evenly dried. The cherries will shrink and shrivel and look a lot like raisins. They should feel leathery and sticky with no damp spots, which will cause them to mold.

To dry mangoes is even easier. Simply peel a ripe mango, slice it into chunks or slices that are about 1/4 inch (6 mm) thick, and spread them out in a single layer on lined dehydrator sheets. Dehydrate them for several hours or overnight. When the mangoes are almost dry, turn the chunks or slices over to ensure they're evenly dried. These will feel leathery but not crispy and should have no damp spots.

Allow the dried cherries and dried mangoes to cool at room temperature for at least an hour. Then store them in a sealed container at room temperature for up to a few weeks.

Many other fruits can be dried in the same way. Apple chunks or slices, banana slices, peach slices, apricot slices, whole blueberries, and even watermelon chunks can be dehydrated into almost candy-like sweet and healthy treats. Before drying, fruit can also be sprinkled with spices such as cinnamon or soaked in lemon or lime juice, for even more flavor.

Sun-Drying Tomatoes

Sun-dried tomatoes can lend a deliciously strong and "cooked" tomato flavor to any raw dish. You can buy them, but they are often not raw. Plus they can be expensive.

Thankfully, sun-dried tomatoes can be made easily and inexpensively in a dehydrator. Farmers' markets and local growers are often a bonanza for bargain tomatoes. Buy them in bulk to save even more.

Dried mangoes and cherries can be used in a variety of recipes and can be stored in a jar or lidded container at room temperature for up to three weeks.

Choose ripe tomatoes without blemishes. Roma (plum) tomatoes work best, but any type can be used. Wash the tomatoes well and slicethem in half.

Spread the tomato halves on an unlined dehydrator sheet in a single layer, making sure they don't overlap.

Dehydrate them at 118°F (48°C) for about twenty-four hours, until the tomatoes are leathery and have no damp or wet spots.

Store the dried tomatoes in glass jars or a lidded container. They will keep at room temperature for up to several weeks or in the freezer for up to several months.

Drying, Freezing, and Storing Herbs

In the summer, we often enjoy an abundance of herbs. Sometimes we grow so many that we couldn't possibly use them all. Drying and freezing herbs can preserve the bounty for later use and be economical as well. Sage, basil, chives, rosemary, mints, lemon balm, cilantro, thyme, bay leaves, parsley, and dill all can be dried or frozen.

Drying Herbs

Dried herbs are usually much stronger than fresh, as much as three to four times as strong. Here's how to dry them.

1. Harvest herbs in the middle of the day, when the morning moisture has dried but the plants haven't begun to wilt.

2. Clean them well and remove any bruised or damaged leaves.

3. Spread the leaves out in a single layer on a lined dehydrator tray.

4. Dehydrate at 118°F (48°C) for 1 to 6 hours until completely dry. The herbs will be dried when they crumble and the stems break easily.

5. Store whole leaves or crumbled ones in air-tight containers, preferably glass. They will retain their freshness for up to a couple months at room temperature or several months in the freezer.

Freezing Herbs

Frozen herbs can be easily added to soups, smoothies, and sauces. Here's how to freeze them.

1. Harvest herbs in the middle of the day, when the morning moisture has dried but the plants haven't begun to wilt.

2. Clean them well and remove any bruised or damaged leaves. Remove most of the hard stems.

3. Chop the leaves coarsely.

4. Spoon the chopped leaves into ice cube trays, packing each cube quite full with herbs.

5. Gently pour water into the herbs until it comes to the top of the tray.

6. Freeze for 24 hours to ensure the cubes are frozen through.

7. When the cubes are frozen solid, remove the herb cubes from the tray and store them in the freezer in an airtight container or plastic bag.

Candying Nuts and Seeds

Candied nuts and seeds are a tasty addition to salads and desserts, and they're super easy to make. See page 48 for some suggested combinations.

You can use any nut, seed, or nut/seed combination. Mix the nuts or seeds with a liquid sweetener such as agave or maple syrup. The ratio is 1 cup (135 to 145 g) nuts/seeds to ¼ cup (60 ml) liquid sweetener.

Add any spices or flavorings.

Stir until the nuts are evenly coated. Spread the nuts or seeds out on lined dehydrator trays and dry for twenty-four hours at 118°F (48°C).

Store the finished candied nuts or seeds in an airtight container, preferably glass, for up to a week.

Maple Cinnamon Almonds and Walnuts

This candied nut combination is sweet and spicy. It's great all by itself as a snack, and it also goes well as an addition to salads or on top of banana ice cream.

- **1 cup (145 g) almonds**
- **1 cup (100 g) walnuts**
- **½ cup (120 ml) maple syrup**
- **1½ teaspoons ground cinnamon**
- **½ teaspoon ground ginger**
- **½ teaspoon salt**

In a medium bowl, mix all of the ingredients together. Spread them out on lined dehydrator trays, and dry for 24 hours at 118°F (48°C).

YIELD: 2 CUPS (240 G)

Sweet Chili Pistachios

Mmm, chili pistachios. Add a bit of cayenne for more heat.

- **2 cups (270 g) shelled pistachios**
- **¼ cup (60 ml) agave**
- **1 teaspoon chili powder**
- **1 teaspoon onion powder**
- **½ teaspoon cumin**
- **½ teaspoon cayenne pepper (optional)**
- **½ teaspoon salt**

In a medium bowl, mix all of the ingredients together. Spread them out on lined dehydrator trays, and dry for 24 hours at 118°F (48°C).

YIELD: 2 CUPS (270 G)

Caramelized Onions

Caramelized onions can be easily made raw using a dehydrator. They are lovely additions to salads and sandwiches.

- **3 cups (480 g) thinly sliced onions**
- **½ cup (120 ml) agave**
- **¼ cup (60 ml) olive oil**
- **½ cup (120 ml) balsamic vinegar**
- **1 teaspoon garlic powder**
- **1 teaspoon salt**

Slice the onions into very thin rounds, and place them in a bowl or container.

In a medium bowl, whisk together the agave, oil, vinegar, garlic powder, and salt. Pour the mixture over the onions. Stir to coat the onions. Let marinate for an hour and then spread out on lined dehydrator sheets. Dry at 118°F (48°C) for 4 to 6 hours, until most of the liquid has evaporated and the onion slices have taken on a slightly brown and cooked appearance.

Store leftovers in a tightly covered container in the refrigerator for up to 3 days.

YIELD: 1½ CUPS (165 G)

Sauerkraut

Cabbage has naturally occurring *Lactobacillus acidophilus,* which is a bacteria that is excellent for gut health and will help the sauerkraut ferment. You can use additional probiotic powder, but it's optional.

- **5 pounds (2.3 kg) shredded cabbage, red or green or a mix of both**
- **2 tablespoons (36 g) salt**
- **1 cup (100 g) chopped scallions (optional)**
- **1 tablespoon (7 g) crushed caraway (optional)**
- **1 tablespoon (10 g) minced garlic (optional)**
- **1 cup (150 g) finely chopped green bell pepper (optional)**
- **1 teaspoon probiotic powder (optional)**

Peel several full leaves from the outside of the cabbage and wash them and set them aside.

Cut the cabbage into wedges. Grate the cabbage using a box grater or the grater plate on your food processor.

Place the grated cabbage in a large bowl, and sprinkle the salt over it. Using your hands, massage the salt into the cabbage until the cabbage is softened, and has reduced in size, and the juices are coming out nicely.

Sauerkraut is delicious on its own, or additions can be made. If desired, mix in your choice of optional additions. Place the cabbage in a very large glass container or a few smaller ones. Press the grated cabbage down and pack it in tightly. This has the added benefit of creating more juicy brine. Pour the juices, known as brine, over the cabbage until it covers the cabbage. It's essential that the cabbage be completely covered with the brine; otherwise it will mold. The cabbage cannot come into contact with the air because it will spoil.

Place a few cabbage leaves over the top of the cabbage in the jar, and then weigh it down to push the cabbage leaf fully under the brine.

Place the jar in a cool, dark room, and allow it to set for about 10 days. Then do a taste test, and see if you like the flavor. Use it at 10 days, or allow it to ferment longer. Once it's reached the perfect flavor, scoop it out into smaller canning jars and place in the refrigerator. Sauerkraut will last for several months when refrigerated.

YIELD: 5 POUNDS (2.3 KG)

Part II

Easy, Affordable Recipes

Smoothies

> **"**Let food be thy medicine, and medicine be thy food.**"** —*Hippocrates*

Smoothies can put you on the right track to superior nutrition and great health. They're simply blended drinks, usually made of a mix of fruits and greens. Any fruits and vegetables can be used, such as strawberries or mangoes or even cucumbers or beets, and the combinations are virtually limitless.

Versatile and convenient, smoothies maximize fruit and vegetable intake and allow you to consume several servings of fruits and vegetables at one meal. They're juicy, and they will help you stay adequately hydrated, too. Increase the nutrition without affecting the taste by using lots of mild-flavored greens, such as spinach and romaine lettuce. Kale is also a great-tasting addition. Dates or a little bit of stevia can provide additional sweetness, if desired.

Smoothies contain lots of nutrients, micronutrients, and antioxidants, and they are also a rich source of fiber, which aids in digestion and helps us feel full. Insoluble fiber, such as that found in broccoli and grains, can help prevent bowel cancers. Soluble fiber, such as that found in beets, peas, beans, and citrus, helps lower blood cholesterol and prevents heart disease.

Begin making smoothies by using approximately half greens and half fruit. For a greener drink, increase the amount of greens and reduce the amount of fruit as your taste adjusts. Fresh and frozen bananas are a delicious and affordable addition to green smoothies and will make them creamy and smooth. Fruits or vegetables in danger of becoming overripe, or surplus fruit purchased in season, can be frozen and used throughout the year as smoothie ingredients.

Basic Green Smoothie

This is the simplest green smoothie, using some leafy greens, a little banana, and optional dates for sweetness. It's a good-for-you-treat that tastes like a sweet, guilty pleasure.

- 2 cups (60 g) chopped spinach or 2 cup (135 g) chopped fresh kale
- 1 large banana, sliced and frozen
- 3 dates, softened in water (optional)
- 1 cup (235 ml) water
- 6 ice cubes

In a blender, puree all ingredients until very smooth.

YIELD: ABOUT THREE 1-CUP (235-ML) SERVINGS

Orange Mango Smoothie

This is a bright and sunny treat that will cheer up any morning and start the day right.

- 1 cup (175 g) mango chunks, frozen
- 1 cup (235 ml) orange juice
- 1 large banana, sliced and frozen
- 3 dates, softened in water (optional)
- 6 ice cubes

Blend all ingredients until very smooth.

YIELD: ABOUT THREE 1-CUP (235-ML) SERVINGS

Raspberry Blast Smoothie

Raspberries are in season starting in early summer and continuing through until late fall. They're delicate berries that don't handle transport well, though, so farmers' markets and local growers are your best bet for the finest and most affordable specimens. Red raspberries will lend a beautiful magenta color to this treat.

- 1 cup (125 g) red raspberries, fresh or frozen, plus additional for topping
- 1 cup (235 ml) orange juice
- 1 banana, sliced and frozen
- 3 tablespoons (50 g) date paste (See recipe on page 130.)
- 6 ice cubes

Blend all ingredients until very smooth. Top with a few fresh raspberries.

YIELD: ABOUT THREE 1-CUP (235-ML) SERVINGS

Nutrition FYI: Spinach and Kale

Spinach and kale are among the most nutrient-dense foods available. Just 1 cup (70 g) of kale will provide as much as 684 percent of the RDA for vitamin K, which is essential for bone and cardiovascular health.

Nutrition FYI: Raspberries

Raspberries contain a phytonutrient called rheosmin, also known as "raspberry ketone." It shows promise in weight loss and the management of obesity.

Smoothie Packs—Just Add Water!

Keeping smoothie packs on hand in the freezer can be a convenient time- and money-saver. Start with the freshest produce and wash and chop as needed. To keep ingredients from sticking together, freeze them in a single layer on a cookie sheet, and then store in freezer bags or boxes until ready to use. When ready to use, just add water, nut milk, or juice (about 1 to 2 cups [235 to 470 ml] per pack, depending on how thick you like it) and blend!

Spicy Spinach Apple

- 3 ounces (85 g) chopped spinach
- 1 medium apple, peeled and chopped
- 1 medium banana, sliced into 1-inch (2.5-cm) chunks
- 1 inch (2.5 cm) piece peeled gingerroot

Strawberry Lime

- 2 cups (110 g) chopped Romaine lettuce
- 1 cup (170 g) sliced strawberries
- 1 banana, sliced into 1-inch (2.5-cm) chunks
- ¼ lime, peeled

Pineapple Kale

- 2 cups (135 g) chopped kale leaves
- 1 cup (165 g) pineapple chunks
- 1 banana, sliced into 1-inch (2.5-cm) chunks

Gone Fruity

- 1 cup (175 g) mango chunks
- ½ cup (85 g) pineapple chunks
- 1 orange, peeled and sectioned
- 1 banana, sliced into 1-inch (2.5-cm) chunks

YIELD: EACH PACK MAKES ABOUT 3 CUPS (700 ML) OF SMOOTHIE

Orange Sunrise

- 1 orange, peeled and frozen
- ½ red or orange bell pepper, chopped
- 1 carrot, peeled and sliced into 1-inch (2.5-cm) pieces
- 1 banana, sliced into 1-inch (2.5-cm) chunks

Tip: Add 1 to 2 tablespoons (6 to 12 g) of chia seeds, ground flax, or hemp protein to any of these smoothies for an extra nutritional boost. A dropper of liquid stevia or a few dates will add a bit more sweetness, if desired.

Chocolate Nut Butter Smoothie

This smoothie reminds me of a frosty peanut butter cup. It's rich and decadent and made to be poured in two or more layers.

For the Chocolate Layer
- **2 bananas, sliced and frozen**
- **¼ cup (35 g) cacao powder**
- **1 cup (235 ml) almond milk or flax milk**

For the Nut Butter Layer
- **2 bananas**
- **¼ cup (65 g) almond butter**
- **1 cup (235 ml) almond milk or flax milk**
- **Chopped almonds, for garnish (optional)**
- **Cacao nibs, for garnish (optional)**

To make the chocolate layer: In a blender, process all the chocolate layer ingredients until very smooth. Pour half into another container and set aside. Divide the remaining smoothie mixture between two glasses.

To make the nut butter layer: Blend the nut butter layer ingredients until very smooth, and divide between the glasses. Spoon this on top of the chocolate layer, being careful not to blend the two layers too much. Then, gently add the remaining chocolate layer mixture.

This is beautiful when made in three layers, but is just as delicious if made in two. Top with chopped almonds and/or cacao nibs, if using.

YIELD: ABOUT 4 CUPS (940 ML)

Cherry Chocolate Layered Smoothie

This smoothie is simple but tasty and visually beautiful. The red cherry layer contrasts perfectly with the dark chocolate layer.

For the Chocolate Layer
- **2 bananas, sliced and frozen**
- **¼ cup (35 g) cacao powder**
- **1 cup (235 ml) almond milk or flax milk**

For the Cherry Layer
- **1 medium banana, sliced and frozen**
- **1 cup (155 g) frozen cherries**
- **1 cup (235 ml) almond milk or flax milk**

To make the cherry layer: In a blender, process all the cherry layer ingredients until smooth and creamy. Divide the mixture evenly, and spoon ontop of the chocolate layer.

To make the chocolate layer: In a blender, process all the chocolate layer ingredients until smooth and creamy. Divide the mixture evenly, and spoon into two glasses.

YIELD: ABOUT 4 CUPS (940 ML)

Watermelon and Strawberry Summer Smoothie

This light and refreshing treat is perfectly cooling on even the hottest summer day.

- **1 cup (150 g) fresh watermelon chunks, frozen**
- **1 cup (255 g) frozen strawberries**
- **3 tablespoons (45 ml) lime juice**
- **1 small bunch fresh mint leaves**
- **1 cup (235 ml) orange juice or water**
- **6 ice cubes**
- **1 or 2 droppers liquid stevia (optional)**
- **Sliced strawberries, for garnish (optional)**
- **Mint leaves, for garnish (optional)**

Blend all ingredients until very smooth. Sweeten with stevia, if using. Garnish with a sliced strawberry and/or mint leaves, if using.

YIELD: ABOUT 3 CUPS (700 ML)

Nutrition FYI: Watermelon

Watermelon is particularly high in the carotenoid phytonutrient lycopene. Contrary to popular belief, the most nutrition is not found in the rind. High levels of nutrition are found throughout the fruit, in the rind, the flesh, and the seeds.

Dreamsicle Smoothie

This smoothie is bursting with orange creaminess, or maybe it's creamy orangeness. Either way, it's delicious and perfect for breakfast, a snack, or an anytime treat.

For the Cream Layer
- **2 bananas, frozen**
- **1 cup (235 ml) almond milk or flax milk**
- **1 teaspoon vanilla extract or 1 teaspoon vanilla powder (See condiments section on page 131.)**

For the Orange Layer
- **2 oranges, peeled, sectioned, and frozen**
- **1 cup (235 ml) carrot juice, almond, or flax milk**
- **2 bananas, frozen**
- **½ teaspoon orange extract (optional)**
- **Chopped almonds, for garnish (optional)**

For the cream layer: In a blender, process all the cream layer ingredients until very smooth. Divide between two large glasses.

To make the orange layer: In the blender, process all the orange layer ingredients until very smooth. Spoon this evenly on top of the cream layer. Add a few chopped almonds to the top, if using.

Option: Make this in several layers or swirl two or more layers together for a pretty presentation.

YIELD: ABOUT 4 CUPS (940 ML)

Double Greens Smoothie

This is a slightly less-sweet smoothie with an emphasis on greens. It's packed with green goodness and is a great start to the day.

- 1 cup (30 g) chopped fresh spinach
- 1 small cucumber, peeled and chopped
- 1 banana, sliced and frozen
- 1 or 2 droppers stevia (optional)
- 1 cup (235 ml) water
- 6 ice cubes

Place all ingredients in a blender and puree until very smooth.

YIELD: ABOUT 4 CUPS (940 ML)

Hemp and Carrot Berry Smoothie

Hemp protein is wonderfully healthy, and full of omega-3 fats, and it will increase daily protein intake considerably.

- ¼ cup (32 g) hemp protein powder
- 1 carrot, peeled and chopped
- 2 cups (135 g) chopped fresh kale
- 1 cup (255 g) frozen strawberries
- 1 banana, sliced and frozen
- 1 cup (235 ml) almond milk, flax milk, or water

Place all ingredients in a blender and puree until very smooth.

YIELD: ABOUT 3½ CUPS (825 ML)

Nutrition FYI: Oranges

Vitamin C is the primary water-soluble antioxidant in the human body. It neutralizes free radicals and reduces DNA damage inside cells. Vitamin C is not stored in the body and must be ingested every day to keep the vitamin at optimal levels. Just one orange provides 116 percent of the daily requirement for vitamin C.

Very Berry Smoothie

This is a favorite, go-to smoothie. It's simple, delicious, and full of the wonderful, protective antioxidants found in berries.

½ cup (75 g) strawberries, fresh or frozen

½ cup (75 g) blueberries, fresh or frozen

½ cup (65 g) raspberries, fresh or frozen

2 bananas, sliced and frozen

3 tablespoons (50 g) date paste or 1 dropper liquid stevia (optional)

1 teaspoon vanilla powder or vanilla extract (optional)

2 cups (470 ml) almond milk, flax milk, or water

6 ice cubes

Additional berries, for garnish (optional)

Blend all ingredients until very smooth. This looks pretty topped with a few whole berries.

YIELD: ABOUT 4 CUPS (940 ML)

Nutritional FYI: Berries

Brightly colored berries aren't only sweet, succulent, and delicious. They also contain vitamin C and powerful antioxidants, such as lutein, anthocyanins, ellagic acid, and quercetin. Great taste, great nutrition.

Strawberry and Lemon Slush

Who needs artificial colors and flavors? Kids and adults will love this cool and refreshingly real, frosty drink.

- 2   **cups (510 g) frozen strawberries**
- 3   **tablespoons (45 ml) lemon juice**
- 1   **teaspoon lemon zest**
- 1   **banana, sliced and frozen**
- 1 or 2   **droppers stevia (optional)**
- 1   **cup (235 ml) water**

Place all ingredients in a blender and puree until very smooth.

YIELD: ABOUT 3 CUPS (700 ML)

Raspberry Aqua Fresca

Chia is wonderfully hydrating when soaked in water and also provides essential fatty acids that are critical for good health.

- ¼   **cup (85 g) chia seeds**
- 2   **cups (470 ml) water**
- 1   **cup (225 g) frozen raspberries**
- 2   **tablespoons (30 ml) lemon juice**
- 2   **droppers liquid stevia (optional)**

Place all ingredients in a blender and puree. Allow to stand for several minutes so the chia has a chance to soak up the water and become a gel.

YIELD: ABOUT 3 CUPS (700 ML)

Watermelon and Lime Slush

The watermelon and lime combine to taste like a delightfully fruity, tropical punch.

- 2   **cups (300 g) watermelon, cut into chunks and frozen**
- ¼   **cup (60 ml) lime juice**
- 1   **teaspoon lime peel**
- 1   **banana, sliced and frozen**
- 1 or 2   **droppers stevia (optional)**
- 1   **cup (235 ml) orange juice or water**

Place all ingredients in a blender and puree until very smooth.

YIELD: ABOUT 3½ CUPS (825 ML)

Nutrition FYI: Chia

Chia is one of the richest sources of omega-3 fatty acids, specifically alpha-linolenic acid, or ALA. It's also rich in fiber, antioxidants, and minerals.

Flavored Waters

Flavored waters are a terrific and tasty way to stay hydrated. They are less sweet than smoothies and use herbs for flavor, but stevia or agave can be added for additional sweetness, if desired.

Watermelon Rosemary

1   cup (150 g) watermelon chunks
2   tablespoons (30 ml) lemon juice
1   tablespoon (2 g) fresh rosemary or 1 teaspoon dried
3   cups (700 ml) water
12 ice cubes

Place the watermelon in a pitcher. Slightly smash the watermelon chunks, and add the lemon juice, rosemary, and water. Allow to stand in the refrigerator for a couple of hours to allow the flavors to develop. Add the ice cubes when ready to serve.

YIELD: ABOUT 5 CUPS (1.2 L)

Strawberry Basil

1   cup (170 g) sliced strawberries
2   tablespoons (30 ml) lemon juice
3   tablespoons (9 g) chopped, fresh basil leaves
3   cups (700 ml) water
12 ice cubes

Put the strawberries, lemon juice, and basil leaves in a pitcher, and mash with a fork or vegetable masher. Add the water and allow it to stand for a couple of hours in the refrigerator for the flavors to develop. Add the ice cubes when ready to serve.

YIELD: ABOUT 5 CUPS (1.2 L)

Blueberry Lemon Mint

1   cup (145 g) fresh blueberries
¼   cup (60 ml) lemon juice
3   tablespoons (18 g) chopped fresh mint leaves
3   cups (700 ml) water
12 ice cubes

Put the blueberries, lemon juice, and mint leaves in a pitcher. Mash with a fork or vegetable masher. Add the water and allow it to stand for a couple of hours for the flavors to develop. Add the ice cubes when ready to serve.

YIELD: ABOUT 5 CUPS (1.2 L)

Pineapple Cucumber

1   cup (165 g) pineapple chunks
1   cup (120 g) cucumber slices
3   fresh sage leaves
3   cups (700 ml) water
12 ice cubes

Put the pineapple, cucumber, and sage leaves in a pitcher, and crush with a fork or vegetable masher. Allow to stand for a couple of hours in the refrigerator for the flavors to develop. Add the ice cubes when ready to serve.

YIELD: ABOUT 6 CUPS (1.4 L)

6

chapter

> **"**But to eat only raw food, you've got to love a salad. You've got to just love a salad.**"**
>
> —*Woody Harrelson, actor*

Salads & Dressings

Salads are a delight to the senses. With their vibrant colors, nearly endless tastes and textures, and enticing aromas, there's nothing boring or mundane about them. They're packed with vitamins and minerals, great taste, and beauty to boot. Even the ancient Romans enjoyed salads made of greens and dressing.

Just adding a salad a day to a normal diet can provide an immediate increase in vitamin, mineral, phytochemical, and fiber intake.

Common salad ingredients are extremely high in vitamin K, which is essential for heart health, as well as vitamins A, C, and E, and minerals such as calcium, iron, potassium, manganese, and copper. Nuts and seeds provide soluble and insoluble fiber, as well as healthy omega-3 fatty acids. It's like a big bowl full of super nutrition.

With a little bit of bargain shopping and planning, salads can be economical, too. Keep a lookout for the freshest produce available when buying ingredients. This will prevent waste and spoilage because the items will last longer.

Clean your produce and store it properly, and it will remain fresher longer. Keeping things ready to go will also make meal-making a snap.

Greens can be gently washed and dried, and then stored wrapped in paper towels inside lidded containers. They should keep for up to a week or even longer.

It can be a good idea to keep commonly used salad toppings handy. Keep a supply of cut-up vegetables, such as carrots, celery, cauliflower, broccoli, and onions, and simply toss a few handfuls onto a bed of greens for a perfect salad. Talk about fast food!

Salads can be served chilled or at room temperature, depending on your taste. Most will be best slightly chilled because it keeps the greens crisp.

Apple Walnut Salad
with Strawberry Vinaigrette Dressing

This colorful salad is an homage to a similar one I regularly enjoy at my favorite local eatery. The apples, berries, and nuts are a triple header of awesome-tasting nutrition.

Nutrition FYI: Strawberries

Just eight strawberries contain 88 milligrams of ascorbic acid. That's 140 percent of the recommended daily allowance for vitamin C. They also contain a good amount of folic acid, which is especially important for pregnant woman, as well as potassium and fiber.

For the Dressing

- 1   cup (145 g) strawberries
- ½   cup (90 g) dates, soaked for at least 30 minutes
- ¼   cup (60 ml) balsamic vinegar
- 1   clove garlic, pressed, or about 1 heaping teaspoon minced garlic
- ½   teaspoon salt
- ½   teaspoon black pepper
- 1   dropper stevia (optional)
- ¼   cup (60 ml) water, more or less, for blending
     salt
     pepper

To make the salad: Arrange the Romaine on two plates and the remaining salad ingredients on top of the Romaine.

To make the dressing: Blend the dressing ingredients until very smooth, and use it to top the salad. Add additional salt and pepper to taste, if needed.

YIELD: 2 SERVINGS

Red Lettuce and Salty Cheese Salad with Sweet French Dressing

Sweet and savory combine perfectly in this salad, and the salty cheese adds another layer of interesting flavor.

For the Salad

- ¾ pound (340 g) red lettuce, torn into large pieces
- ½ cup (80 g) sliced red onion
- ½ cup (50 g) sliced green or black olives
- 1 cup (145 g) sunflower seed sprouts (See how-to on page 40.)
- ½ cup (60 g) Salty Cheese, chopped into bits (See recipe on page 140.)

For the Sweet French Dressing

- 1 cup (180 g) chopped tomatoes
- ½ cup (40 g) sundried tomatoes, soaked in water for 30 minutes
- 6 dates, soaked in water for 30 minutes
- ½ cup (120 ml) orange juice
- 2 tablespoons (20 g) chopped onion
- 1 teaspoon minced fresh garlic
- 1 teaspoon ground paprika
- 3 tablespoons (45 ml) apple cider vinegar
- 1 teaspoon salt
- ½ teaspoon black pepper

To make the salad: Assemble all the salad ingredients on two salad plates.

To make the dressing: Puree all the dressing ingredients in a blender until very smooth. Pour on the salad.

Leftover dressing can be stored in a covered container in the refrigerator for up to a few days.

YIELD: 2 LARGE SALADS AND ABOUT 2 CUPS (470 ML) DRESSING

Massaged Lemony Kale

By nearly every measure, kale is tops for nutrition. It has plentiful vitamin K, as well as vitamins A and C. It also has minerals such as iron, calcium, potassium, copper, and manganese. Massaging the greens helps soften them, making them even more palatable and delicious.

¼   cup (60 ml) olive oil
¼   cup (60 ml) lemon juice
2   tablespoons (30 ml) agave
1   teaspoon minced fresh garlic
½   teaspoon salt
½   teaspoon black pepper
1   pound (455 g) fresh chopped kale
6   scallions, sliced

In a small bowl, whisk together the oil, lemon juice, agave, garlic, salt, and pepper. Pour over the chopped kale. Use your hands to rub and massage the dressing into the kale leaves. Once the leaves are softened slightly, which will only take a few minutes, stir in the sliced scallions.

YIELD: 2 SERVINGS

Arugula and Mustard Greens Salad with Creamy Avocado Dill Dressing

The spicy hot greens in this salad are chilled down by the Creamy Avocado Dill Dressing.

For the Salad

4   cups (80 g) arugula
1   cup (55 g) mustard greens, chopped
1   small cucumber, sliced
1   small yellow onion, sliced thinly

For the Dressing

1   avocado, chopped (about 1 cup [145 g])
1   tablespoon (10 g) chopped onion
1   teaspoon minced fresh garlic
1   tablespoon (15 ml) agave
3   tablespoons (45 ml) lemon juice
1   tablespoon (15 ml) apple cider vinegar
½   cup (120 ml) almond milk, flax milk, or water
1   teaspoon salt
½   teaspoon black pepper
2   teaspoons dried dill or 2 tablespoons (4 g) fresh dill

To make the salad: Assemble all the salad ingredients on two salad plates.

To make the dressing: Puree all the dressing ingredients, except for the dill, in a blender until very smooth. Add the dill, and stir well before serving.

Leftover dressing can be stored in a covered container in the refrigerator for up to a few days.

YIELD: 2 LARGE SALADS AND ABOUT 2¾ CUPS (530 ML) DRESSING

Green Lettuce and Dates with Sweet Apple Dressing

Beautiful fruits, tender greens, and a sweet apple dressing go together perfectly in this refreshing salad.

For the Salad

- ¾ pound (340 g) green leaf lettuce
- 1 apple, sliced thinly
- ½ cup (90 g) chopped dates
- ½ cup (55 g) pecans
- 4 scallions, sliced

For the Dressing

- 1 cup (150 g) peeled and chopped apple
- 3 dates, soaked in water for 30 minutes and drained
- 2 tablespoons (30 ml) agave
- 3 tablespoons (45 ml) olive oil
- 2 tablespoons (30 ml) lemon juice
- 1 tablespoon (10 g) chopped onion
- 1 teaspoon minced fresh garlic
- ½ teaspoon ground cinnamon
- ¼ teaspoon ground nutmeg
- ½ teaspoon salt
- ½ teaspoon black pepper

To make the salad: Make a bed of greens and layer on the remaining ingredients.

To make the dressing: Puree all the dressing ingredients in a blender until very smooth, and dress the salad.

Leftover dressing can be stored in a covered container in the refrigerator for up to a few days.

YIELD: 2 LARGE SALADS AND ABOUT 1½ CUPS (355 ML) DRESSING

Grapefruit Pear and Candied Nut Salad with Orange Dressing

Pears go deliciously well in this salad. The candied nuts add crunchy little nuggets of spicy sweetness.

For the Salad

- **1 large grapefruit, peeled and cut into sections**
- **1 head Romaine lettuce**
- **1 pear, sliced thinly**
- **3 scallions, sliced**
- **¼ cup (35 g) candied nuts**
- **¼ cup (45 g) raisins or chopped dates**

For the Dressing

- **1 cup (235 ml) orange juice**
- **4 dates, soaked in the orange juice for 30 minutes**
- **¼ cup (60 ml) olive oil**
- **2 tablespoons (30 ml) apple cider vinegar**
- **1 tablespoon (10 g) chopped onion**
- **1 teaspoon minced fresh garlic**
- **1 teaspoon salt**
- **½ teaspoon black pepper**

To make the salad: Peel and section the grapefruit (See "How to Cut and Section a Grapefruit," page 30). Begin by cutting ¼ inch (6 mm) of the ends off the grapefruit so that it will rest flat. Then slice the skin off from top to bottom, following the round contour of the grapefruit, and only cutting away as much as necessary so nothing is wasted. Use a sharp knife to remove each grapefruit section from the remaining membrane. Assemble the salad and add the grapefruit sections.

To make the dressing: Puree all the dressing ingredients in a blender until very smooth.

Leftover dressing can be stored in a covered container in the refrigerator for up to a few days.

YIELD: 2 LARGE SALADS AND ABOUT 1½ CUPS (355 ML) DRESSING

Romaine Broccoli and Caramelized Onion with Lemon Tahini Dressing

The star of this salad is the Lemon Tahini Dressing, which is creamy and delightful but strong enough to stand up to the powerful flavors of the onion and broccoli.

For the Salad

- 1 head Romaine lettuce
- 1 cup (70 g) broccoli florets
- ¾ cup (102 g) caramelized onions (See how-to on page 48.)

For the Dressing

- ¼ cup (60 ml) lemon juice
- 1 teaspoon lemon peel
- 4 dates, soaked in water for 30 minutes
- ½ cup (120 g) tahini
- ¼ to ½ cup (60 to 120 ml) water, depending on desired consistency
- 1 teaspoon fresh minced garlic
- 1 tablespoon (15 ml) apple cider vinegar
- 1 tablespoon (15 ml) soy sauce
- ½ teaspoon salt

To make the salad: Assemble all the salad ingredients on two salad plates.

To make the dressing: Puree all the dressing ingredients in a blender until very smooth and dress the salad.

Leftover dressing can be stored in a covered container in the refrigerator for up to a few days.

YIELD: 2 LARGE SALADS AND ABOUT 1¼ CUPS (295 ML) DRESSING

Nutrition FYI: Hot Peppers

Hot peppers such as cayenne and the jalapenos used to make chipotle seasoning contain capsaicin, which is a powerful anti-inflammatory. Inflammation is implicated in many health problems, and eating foods that reduce inflammation can be protective and preventive.

Baby Greens and Mango Lime Chipotle Dressing

Baby arugula works especially well in this sweet and flavorful salad.

For the Salad

¾	pound (340 g) baby greens
½	cup (80 g) thinly sliced red onion
¼	cup (25 g) walnuts

For the Dressing

1	cup (175 g) mango chunks
¼	cup (60 ml) lime juice
¼	cup (60 g) tahini
3	tablespoons (45 ml) agave or maple syrup
1	teaspoon minced fresh garlic
1	tablespoon (10 g) chopped onion
½ to 1	teaspoon chipotle powder

To make the salad: Assemble the salad ingredients on two salad plates.

To make the dressing: Puree all the dressing ingredients in a blender until very smooth and dress the salad.

Leftover dressing can be stored in a covered container in the refrigerator for up to a few days.

YIELD: 2 LARGE SALADS AND ABOUT 1½ CUPS (355 ML) DRESSING

Avocado Mango and Sprout Salad with Fat-Free Sweet and Spicy Mango Dressing

Sunflower sprouts add a fresh crunch, and the avocados and mushrooms add substance to this hearty salad that is perfect for either lunch or dinner.

For the Salad

1	head Romaine lettuce, torn into pieces
1	avocado, sliced
1	cup (70 g) sliced mushrooms
1½	cups (265 g) mango chunks
3	scallions, sliced
½	cup (50 g) walnuts
1	cup (45 g) sunflower sprouts (See how-to on page 40.)

For the Dressing

1	cup (175 g) chopped mango
½	cup (35 g) sun-dried tomatoes, soaked in water for 30 minutes (See how-to on page 44.)
6	dates, soaked in water for 30 minutes
2	tablespoons (30 ml) agave
1	teaspoon minced fresh garlic
1	tablespoon (15 ml) apple cider vinegar
1	cup (235 ml) water
1	teaspoon ground paprika
¼ to ½	teaspoon cayenne pepper
1	tablespoon (10 g) minced onion
½	teaspoon salt
½	teaspoon black pepper

To make the salad: Assemble the salad by making a bed of Romaine two salad plates and arranging the remaining salad ingredients on top.

To make the dressing: Place all the dressing ingredients in a blender and puree until very smooth. Drizzle over the salad when ready to serve.

Leftover dressing can be stored in a covered container in the refrigerator for up to a few days.

YIELD: 2 LARGE SALADS AND ABOUT 2½ CUPS (590 ML) DRESSING

Salad in a Jar: Romaine Tomato Olive with Easy Italian Dressing

A salad in a jar can be a convenient way to bring a super-healthy lunch or snack to work or school. You'll need two 24-ounce (710-ml) glass jars with lids for this salad. The dressing is kept away from the more delicate ingredients by putting the more sturdy items on the bottom of the jars. When you're ready for a salad, just pour it out into a serving bowl and enjoy!

For the Dressing

- ½ cup (120 ml) olive oil
- ¼ cup (60 ml) apple cider vinegar
- 1 tablespoon (15 ml) agave
- 1 tablespoon (3 g) finely minced fresh basil or 1 teaspoon dried basil
- ½ teaspoon dried oregano
- ½ teaspoon thyme
- 1 tablespoon (4 g) finely chopped fresh minced parsley
- 1 teaspoon minced fresh garlic
- ¼ teaspoon celery salt
- ½ teaspoon salt
- ½ teaspoon black pepper

For the Salad

- ½ cup (35 g) sliced mushrooms
- 12 whole cherry tomatoes
- ½ cup (50 g) black olives, sliced
- 3 scallions, sliced thinly
- 4 cups (220 g) Romaine lettuce, chopped

To make the dressing: Make the dressing first. Whisk together all the ingredients until the oil and vinegar are emulsified. Pour about half of the dressing into the bottom of each jar.

To make the salad: In each jar, layer in the mushrooms, tomatoes, olives, and scallions, in that order. The harder vegetables will rest in the bottom with the dressing, and the more tender greens will stay high and dry. Fill the rest of the jar with the Romaine. When ready to serve, just pour the entire contents of the jar out into a bowl.

Salad in a jar can be kept refrigerated for up to 3 days.

YIELD: TWO 24-OUNCE (710 ML) JARS

Salad in a Jar: Iceberg with Creamy Ranch Dressing

Contrary to popular belief, iceberg lettuce is chock full of healthy nutrients, such as vitamins K and A. It's also a classic and timeless ingredient, giving this new twist on salad a traditional feel. Two 24-ounce (710-ml) glass jars with lids are necessary to make this salad.

For the Dressing

- ½ cup (75 g) cashews, soaked for 30 minutes and drained
- 1 tablespoon (15 ml) lemon juice
- 1 tablespoon (15 ml) apple cider vinegar
- ¾ cup (175 ml) water
- 1 teaspoon minced fresh garlic
- 1 tablespoon (1 g) parsley flakes
- 1 tablespoon (3 g) chopped fresh chives
- ½ teaspoon dried dill
- ½ teaspoon salt
- ½ teaspoon black pepper

For the Salad

- ½ cup (50 g) chopped cauliflower
- ½ cup (75 g) thinly sliced red bell pepper
- 5 radishes, thinly sliced
- 3 scallions, thinly sliced
- 4 cups (220 g) chopped iceberg lettuce

To make the dressing: Place the cashews, lemon juice, apple cider vinegar, and water into a blender and puree until everything is very smooth and creamy. Add in the remaining dressing ingredients and pulse a few times to incorporate. Pour about ½ cup (120 ml) into each jar.

To make the salad: In the jar, layer in the cauliflower, pepper, radishes, and scallions. Add the lettuce, and place the lid on the jar. Keep the jar in the refrigerator until ready to serve. Just pour out into a bowl and enjoy!

Salad in a jar can be kept refrigerated for up to 3 days.

YIELD: TWO 24-OUNCE (710-ML) JARS

Tip: This ranch dressing is customizable in nearly endless ways. Make this your own by adding in some lemon peel, cayenne, paprika, or curry powder. Make enough for a crowd by doubling or tripling the recipe.

Dressings

These dressings go well with just about any salad combination. Double or triple the recipes and store in a glass jar in the refrigerator for up to a week.

The Best Salad Dressing Ever (Really!)

This is the best salad dressing ever (really!) and gets rave reviews without fail. It goes especially well with baby arugula or other tender greens.

- 1 **cup (235 ml) olive oil**
- ¼ **cup (60 ml) lemon juice**
- 1 **tablespoon (6 g) lemon zest**
- 1 **tablespoon (10 g) minced onion**
- ¼ **cup plus 2 tablespoons (88 ml) agave**
- 3 **tablespoons (45 ml) soy sauce**
- 3 **tablespoons (35 g) Dijon mustard**
- 3 **tablespoons (45 ml) caper brine**
- 2 **teaspoons minced fresh garlic**
- ¼ **cup plus 2 tablespoons (37 g) chopped black olives**
- ¼ **cup plus 2 tablespoons (50g) capers**

Place all the ingredients in a blender or food processor and pulse several times until the dressing is mixed well and the olives and capers are mostly pulverized.

YIELD: 1¾ CUPS (410 ML) DRESSING

Sweet Green Dressing

Arugula is one of the healthiest greens around and adds an interesting, peppery flavor to this unique green dressing. Use it on any salad to add even more flavor and nutrition. It goes especially well drizzled over tomatoes.

1 cup (20 g) chopped arugula leaves, packed
1 cup (60 g) chopped fresh parsley leaves, packed
¾ cup (175 ml) olive oil
¼ cup (60 ml) agave
¼ cup (60 ml) balsamic vinegar
3 tablespoons (45 ml) lemon juice
1 teaspoon minced fresh garlic
½ teaspoon salt
½ teaspoon ground black pepper
1 tablespoon (10 g) finely minced onion

Place all ingredients in a blender and puree until very smooth.

Store any leftover dressing in a lidded container in the refrigerator for up to 1 week.

YIELD: ABOUT 2½ CUPS (590 ML) DRESSING

Thousand Island

Thousand Island dressing is another traditional favorite. This is great on any salad and also spectacular as a dressing for wraps and a spread for burgers.

1 cup (145 g) cashews, soaked for 30 minutes and drained
1 medium tomato, quartered and seeded
½ cup (40 g) sun-dried tomatoes, soaked for 30 minutes and drained
¼ cup (40 g) chopped red bell pepper
1 teaspoon minced fresh garlic
2 tablespoons (30 ml) apple cider vinegar
2 tablespoons (30 ml) lemon juice
2 tablespoons (30 ml) agave
1 teaspoon ground paprika
1 teaspoon salt
½ teaspoon black pepper
1 cup (235 ml) water
1 tablespoon (10 g) finely minced onion
1 to 2 tablespoons (15 to 30 g) Sweet Pickle Relish (See page 129.), optional

Place all the ingredients, except for the minced onion, in a blender and puree until very smooth and creamy. This will take a minute or two, depending on your machine. Stir in the minced onion. Stir in the Sweet Pickle Relish, if using.

Store any leftover dressing in a lidded container in the refrigerator for up to 1 week.

YIELD: ABOUT 2¾ CUPS (650 ML) DRESSING

chapter

Soups

> **"**Only the pure in heart can make a good soup.**"**
>
> *—Ludwig van Beethoven, German composer and pianist*

Soups are satisfying and comforting in a way few other foods are. They're also a familiar food; we all grew up having soup for lunch. One of my favorite food memories is having tomato soup in the school cafeteria!

Raw soups are often blended and can be much like a savory smoothie. This makes them creamy and delicious and is also helpful in breaking down the cell walls of the plant foods so the nutrients are more available.

According to food historians, soup is probably as old as food preparation itself. We've been combining food ingredients into tasty and nutritious combinations since the beginning.

Just about any cooked soup can be made into a raw version. These soups can be creamy and filling and can easily be warmed in the dehydrator or in a warm pan. Gazpacho and fruit soups are also quite tasty and interesting.

Broccoli Soup

This broccoli soup is made even more hearty and flavorful by optionally marinating and dehydrating the vegetables beforehand.

- **1   pound (455 g) broccoli**
- **½   cup (80 g) chopped onion**
- **3   tablespoons (45 ml) balsamic vinegar**
- **3   tablespoons (45 ml) agave or maple syrup**
- **3   tablespoons (45 ml) olive or flax oil**
- **1   clove garlic**
- **½   teaspoon salt**
- **½   teaspoon black pepper**
- **¼   teaspoon fresh basil**
- **1   cup (145 g) chopped avocado**
- **2   cups (470 ml) water**
- **¼   cup (25 g) chopped scallions**
- **1   teaspoon crushed red-pepper flakes**

Chop the broccoli and add it, along with the onion, to a container. In a bowl, whisk together the vinegar, agave, oil, and garlic, and pour over the broccoli and onion. Spread the broccoli and onion on a lined dehydrator tray, and dehydrate for about two hours at 118 degrees (48°C). If you don't want to use a dehydrator, just skip this step and don't dehydrate anything. It's still a delicious soup.

Remove from the dehydrator, and place the softened broccoli and onions in a blender along with the remaining ingredients. Puree until very smooth and creamy.

Pour into 2 or 3 soup bowls, and garnish with a few chopped scallions and crushed red-pepper flakes.

YIELD: ABOUT 4 CUPS (940 ML)

Cream of Tomato Soup

Because they are meatier, Roma (plum) tomatoes are ideal for this rich and slightly sweet variation of an old favorite. But use any tomatoes that are available.

- **3   medium Roma tomatoes (about 1½ cups [270 g] chopped), plus additional for garnish**
- **3   tablespoons (8 g) fresh basil or 1 tablespoon (2 g) dried basil**
- **1   clove garlic or 1 teaspoon minced garlic**
- **3   dates, softened in water**
- **1½ cups (355 ml) almond milk**
- **¼   cup (60 ml) olive oil**
-     **Salt, to taste**
-     **Black pepper, to taste**
-     **Crushed red-pepper flakes, to taste**

In a blender, puree the tomatoes, basil, garlic, dates, almond milk, and oil until very smooth and creamy. Add salt and pepper to taste, and top with a little chopped tomato, a few crushed red-pepper flakes, and a drizzle of oil.

YIELD: ABOUT 2 SERVINGS

Nutrition FYI: Tomatoes
Tomatoes are a rich source of the potent antioxidant lycopene, thought to prevent many cancers.

Spicy Mango and Cucumber Soup with "Noodles"

This is sweet, savory, and surprisingly filling, and the noodles add an interesting crunch.

- 1 cup (175 g) peeled and chopped mango
- ½ cup (70 g) avocado
- 1 cup (120 g) chopped cucumber
- 3 tablespoons (30 g) chopped onion
- 1 clove garlic or 1 teaspoon minced garlic
- 1 teaspoon minced jalapeño pepper
- 3 dates, softened in water
- 1 cup (235 ml) water more or less, for blending
- 1 small cucumber, cut into "noodles"
- Salt, to taste
- Black pepper, to taste
- Crushed red-pepper flakes, to taste
- 2 teaspoons olive oil

In a blender, process the mango, avocado, cucumber, onion, garlic, jalapeño, dates, and water until very smooth and creamy.

Use a knife or spiral slicer to cut the cucumber into strips (noodles), and add to the soup. Add salt and pepper to taste, and add some crushed red-pepper flakes and a drizzle of oil.

YIELD: ABOUT 2 SERVINGS

Creamy Garlic and Greens Soup

Garlic and greens are super healthy and taste great, too!

- **4** cups (270 g) chopped fresh kale
- **1** avocado, chopped
- **2** cloves garlic
- **3** tablespoons (45 ml) agave
- **½** teaspoon salt
- **½** teaspoon black pepper
- **2** cups (470 ml) almond milk or water
- **¼** cup sliced scallions
- **¼** cup chopped broccoli

Place the kale, avocado, garlic, agave, salt, and pepper, and milk or water in a blender and puree until very smooth. Garnish with sliced scallions and chopped broccoli.

YIELD: 2½ CUPS (625 G)

Carrot Cauliflower and Pear Soup

Cauliflower and other plants in the brassica family (broccoli, kale, cabbage, etc.), extremely important for good health, especially cancer prevention and hormone metabolism. This group of foods contains indole-3 carbinol and sulforaphane, both of which aid healthy estrogen metabolism. Because of that, broccoli is often touted as a breast cancer preventive. This soup is a healthy and easy way to get those preventive ingredients.

- **1** cup (100 g) cauliflower
- **1** cup (170 g) chopped pear
- **4** carrots
- **1** cup (145 g) chopped avocado
- **1** clove garlic
- **1½** cups (355 ml) almond milk plus more for blending
- **½** teaspoon salt
- **½** teaspoon black pepper
- **1** teaspoon crushed red-pepper flakes
  Sunflower seed sprouts
  Small drizzle olive oil or flaxseed oil

In a blender, process the cauliflower, pear, carrots, avocado, garlic, and almond milk on high speed until very smooth.

Add more almond milk or water if necessary for blending. Pour into bowls, and add the salt, pepper, a bit of red-pepper flakes, and a handful of seed sprouts for crunch. Add a small drizzle of olive or flaxseed oil on the top.

YIELD: 3 CUPS (750 G)

Cherry/Tomato Gazpacho

No, not "cherry tomato" gazpacho. Cherries *and* tomatoes are used in this soup. The cherry and tomato combination is interesting and complex. The cherries are sweet and tart at the same time, and the heat from the jalapeños really enhances the flavor, plus this soup goes together in no time at all.

- 2 cups (360 g) chopped tomatoes
- 1 cup (155 g) chopped cherries
- 3 tablespoons (30 g) minced onion
- 1 tablespoon (9 g) finely minced jalapeño pepper, ribs and seeds removed
- 3 tablespoons (30 g) finely minced green or red bell pepper
- 1 teaspoon minced fresh garlic
- 3 tablespoons (18 g) chopped scallions
- 1 teaspoon salt
- ½ teaspoon black pepper, plus additional for garnish
- 1 teaspoon crushed red-pepper flakes, plus additional for garnish

Place the tomatoes and cherries in a food processor fitted with an "S" blade. Pulse them a few times until they are chopped and a little juicy, but stop before they are pureed. This needs to be a little chunky.

Add in the remaining ingredients, and pulse several times until well incorporated. Pour into bowls, and garnish with a little more black pepper and some red-pepper flakes.

YIELD: 2 SERVINGS

Nutrition FYI: Fruit

Fruit is loaded with vitamins, minerals, phytonutrients, bioflavonoids, and antioxidants that build immunity and help prevent cancer and heart disease. Rich in vitamin C, they help keep your blood pressure low, fight free radicals, and help repair damaged cells.

chapter

8

> **"All happiness depends on a leisurely breakfast."**
> —*John Gunther, author and journalist*

Breakfasts

Breakfast means just that: After going many hours without food, the body must "break its fast." So the first meal of the day is of utmost importance. It can be something light or a little more substantial.

Traditional breakfasts vary by country and region. In many parts of the world, breakfast is often cereal, oatmeal, or pancakes. Those are all meals that can be deliciously recreated in raw versions. And we don't have to limit ourselves to imitations of traditional breakfast foods. How about a salad for breakfast? Or pie! Yes, let's have pie for breakfast! Why not? A raw vegan pie is full of nutritious ingredients, mostly fruit, nuts, and dates.

Raw foods can be an opportunity to think differently about food in general, adjust our expectations and traditions, and think outside the box. Smoothies are an excellent way to start the day, as are buckwheat or chia porridges. But savory and salty things can be delicious for the first meal, too.

After sleeping for several hours, replenishing hydration by drinking water is absolutely vital first thing in the morning, even more so than food. Start your day off right with 32 to 48 ounces (960 to 1440 ml) of water. Add a tablespoon of lemon or lime juice and even a little bit of stevia.

Morning Chia Drink

This juicy drink will get you rehydrated and gently fed in the morning as you "break your fast."

- ¼ **cup (25 g) ground chia seeds**
- 4 **cups (940 ml) water**
- 2 **tablespoons (30 ml) lemon or lime juice**
- 1 **dropper stevia**

Pour all ingredients in a large glass or jar and stir immediately and well. Allow to stand for several minutes to allow the chia seeds to gel. This drink is best fresh, but it can be stored in the refrigerator for up to a day or two.

YIELD: ABOUT 4 CUPS (940 ML)

Nutrition FYI: Water
Water removes waste from the body, regulates temperature, lubricates and cushions joints, aids digestion, carries nutrients and oxygen to cells, and maintains the health and integrity of every cell in the body.

Apple Stacks

This simple and fun apple dish is perfect for breakfast.

- ¼ **cup (60 g) almond butter**
- 3 **tablespoons (50 g) date paste**
- 3 **tablespoons (45 ml) almond milk**
- 2 **apples**
- ½ **teaspoon vanilla extract**
  Pinch salt
- 2 **tablespoons (15 g) chopped almonds or walnuts**

In a bowl, mix together the almond butter, date paste, and almond milk until it's a thick paste.

Using an apple corer or a thin sharp knife, core the apples and then slice them into five or six slices. Spread a dab of the almond butter and date paste mix on each layer, sprinkle a few nuts on, and stack the layers.

Apple stacks are best served immediately and don't keep well.

YIELD: 2 APPLE STACKS

Nutrition FYI: Apples
In addition to soluble fiber and vitamin C, apple skins also contain ursolic acid, which may increase muscle and brown fat as well as decrease white fat and obesity.

Lemon Poppy Seed Buckwheat Pancakes

These pancakes are perfect for breakfast or brunch. They taste a lot like lemon poppy seed muffins. Serve them with agave or date syrup.

- 1 **cup (100 g) ground buckwheat groats, soaked and dried**
- ½ **cup (50 g) ground flaxseeds**
- **Pinch salt**
- ½ **cup (115 g) apple puree**
- 3 **tablespoons (45 ml) lemon juice**
- 1 **teaspoon lemon zest**
- ¼ **cup (60 ml) agave**
- 3 **tablespoons (30 g) date paste**
- ¼ **cup (60 ml) water**
- 2 **tablespoons (15 g) poppy seeds**

In a medium bowl, mix together the buckwheat, flaxseeds, and salt. Add the apple puree and then the lemon juice, lemon zest, agave, date paste, and water. Stir until well combined. Fold in the poppy seeds.

Using about 3 tablespoons (45 ml) of batter for each pancake, scoop out pancakes onto a lined dehydrator tray, making 2- to 3-inch (5- to 7.5 cm) rounds that are about ½-inch (1-cm) thick.

Dehydrate at 118°F (48°C) for 6 hours. Peel from the tray liner and flip over onto an unlined dehydrator tray. Continue drying until the outside is beginning to get a little crisp and the inside is still a bit mushy.

Pancakes are best straight out of the dehydrator, but they can be kept in a lidded container in the refrigerator for up to a few days.

YIELD: 4 TO 6 PANCAKES

Nutrition FYI: Buckwheat

Buckwheat isn't a grain. It's a fruit seed related to rhubarb and sorrel. It's high in manganese, tryptophan, magnesium, copper, and fiber, and it has been linked to a lower total serum cholesterol, lower LDL cholesterol, and lower blood pressure. Buckwheat works in synergy with vitamin C and contains flavonoids and antioxidants.

Chia Porridge with Fruit and Nuts

Chia seeds will help you control hunger and keep you feeling full. They also provide super healthy nutrients, such as omega-3 fatty acids and antioxidants.

- ¼ cup (25 g) ground chia seeds
- 1 cup (235 ml) almond or flax milk
- 1 tablespoon (15 ml) agave
- ¼ cup (45 g) sliced strawberries
- ¼ cup (40 g) blueberries
- ¼ cup (45 g) chopped dates
- ¼ cup (25 g) chopped pecans or walnuts

Soak the chia in the almond or flax milk for 30 minutes or overnight. Stir in the agave and adjust to taste. Top with the strawberries, blueberries, dates, and nuts. Store leftovers in a covered container in the refrigerator for 1 to 2 days.

YIELD: 1 SERVING

Fruit Wrap Ups

This is fast food. A few pieces of fruit, a lettuce leaf for wrapping, and a sweet dressing, and you've got a light a refreshing breakfast.

- ½ cup (85 g) sliced mango
- ½ cup (75 g) sliced banana
- ½ cup (70 g) sliced avocado
- 6 Romaine lettuce leaves
- 3 tablespoons (45 ml) orange juice
- 2 tablespoons (30 ml) agave
- 1 tablespoon (15 ml) olive oil
  Salt, to taste
  Black pepper, to taste

Place the mango, banana, and avocado lengthwise in lettuce leaves.

In a small bowl, whisk together the orange juice, agave, and oil and drizzle in each wrap. Season to taste with salt and pepper.

These wraps are best enjoyed right away, but they can be stored in the refrigerator for a day or so.

YIELD: 4 TO 6 WRAPS

Tip: If your mornings are rushed, soak the ground chia in almond milk overnight and chop the fruit and nuts beforehand as well. Then enjoy an instant breakfast the next morning.

Fruit Salad with Sweet Lime Dressing

This fruit salad will start any day off right with juicy delectable fruit and a sweet citrus dressing.

For the Salad
- 1 **cup (55 g) chopped Romaine lettuce**
- 2 **medium oranges, peeled and sectioned**
- 1 **cup (170 g) sliced strawberries**
- 1 **cup (150 g) sliced bananas**

For the Dressing
- ¼ **cup (60 ml) lime juice**
- 3 **tablespoons (45 ml) agave**
- 2 **tablespoons (30 ml) olive oil**
- ½ **teaspoon salt**

For the Topping
- 2 **tablespoons (10 g) finely shredded dried coconut**

Arrange the Romaine on two plates. Evenly divide the fruit and arrange on top of the Romaine.

In a bowl, whisk together the dressing ingredients and pour over both salads. Sprinkle the coconut on top as a garnish. Store leftovers in a covered container in the refrigerator for 1 to 2 days.

YIELD: 2 SALADS

Nutrition FYI: Lime
Limes are alkalizing and contain a good amount of vitamin C. They also contain folate, thiamin, vitamin E, and small amounts of calcium.

Trail Mix Bars

Perfect for breakfast, or even a dessert, this energy bar covers all the nutritional bases and will keep you fueled for hours. Wrap them individually for an anytime treat.

- ¾ cup (105 g) almonds, soaked and dried
- 1½ cups (270 g) dates
- ½ cup (80 g) dried cherries (See page 44 for how to.)
- ½ cup (80 g) dried mango (See page 44 for how to.)
- ½ cup (65 g) sunflower seeds
- ½ cup (50 g) pepitas (hulless pumpkin seeds)
- 3 tablespoons (30 g) cacao nibs

In a food processor fitted with an "S" blade, process the almonds and dates until they are well chopped and begin to stick together. Add the cherries and mango and pulse a few times to incorporate. Add the sunflower seeds, pepitas, and cacao nibs and pulse until just combined.

Press the mixture into an 8" × 8" (20 × 20 cm) container and then turn out onto a board. Cut into 3-inch (7.5 cm) squares.

Wrap them and store in the refrigerator for 1 week or in the freezer for several months.

YIELD: NINE 3-INCH (7.5 CM) SQUARES

Raspberry Buckwheat Crumble Bars

These flavorful energy bars are quick and easy to make. They store beautifully for tomorrow's breakfast or an anytime snack. Wrap them individually for a super convenient snack on the go.

- 1 cup (100 g) buckwheat groats, soaked and dried
- 1½ cups (270 g) chopped dates
- 1 cup (85 g) finely shredded dried coconut
- ½ cup (40 g) dried raspberries (See dried cherries recipe on page 44.)
- ½ cup (55 g) chopped almonds

In a food processor fitted with an "S" blade, process the buckwheat, dates, and coconut until they are chopped, well mixed, and are beginning to stick together. Add the raspberries and almonds and pulse a few times until they're evenly distributed.

Press firmly into a 6" × 6" inch (15 cm × 15 cm) pan or container, then turn out onto a board. Cut into nine 2-inch (5 cm) squares. Wrap them and store in the refrigerator for 1 week or in the freezer for several months.

YIELD: NINE 2-INCH (5 CM) SQUARES

Nutrition FYI: Raspberries

Raspberries are high in fiber, vitamin C, manganese, anthocyanin pigments, ellagic acid, quercetin, and carotenoids, which are antioxidants, and known to prevent various illnesses.

Nutrition FYI: Almonds

Just an ounce of almonds contains 12 percent of the recommended daily amount of protein. They also contain vitamin E, B vitamins, minerals, and healthy fats. They may offer benefits such as clearer skin, improved cholesterol, and a lower risk of some cancers.

Almond Vanilla Dried Cherry Cereal

Crunchy and full of flavor, this raw cereal is also healthier and more economical than commercial granola.

- ½ cup (75 g) almonds, chopped
- ½ cup (80 g) dried cherries
- ½ cup (50 g) buckwheat groats, soaked and dried
- ¼ cup (45 g) chopped dates
- 1 cup (235 ml) sweetened almond or flax milk
- ½ vanilla extract

Divide the almonds between two bowls. Divide the cherries, buckwheat, and dates between the two bowls.

In a small bowl, mix the almond or flax milk with the vanilla and pour over the cereal.

Store the dry cereal without milk added for several weeks in the refrigerator.

YIELD: 3 SERVINGS

Fruit Cereal

Simple chopped fruit is always beautiful and satisfying.

- 1 cup (170 g) sliced peaches (1-inch [2.5 cm] pieces)
- 1 cup (145 g) strawberries, sliced
- 1 banana, sliced into ½-inch (1.3 cm) pieces
- ¼ cup (25 g) walnuts, chopped
- ½ cup (40 g) finely shredded dried coconut
- 2 cups (470 ml) almond or flax milk

Divide the fruit into two bowls. Pour the milk over when ready to serve and enjoy. Store leftover fruit cereal, separate from the milk, in lidded containers in the refrigerator for a day or two.

YIELD: 2 SERVINGS

Chia Cherry Energy Bars

This sweet energy bar, with chewy dried cherries, is quick, easy, and delicious. The chia seeds add a delightful crunch!

1   **cup (330 g) chia seeds**
1   **cup (180 g) chopped dates**
1   **teaspoon vanilla extract**
½   **cup (80 g) dried cherries**

In a food processor fitted with an "S" blade, process the chia seeds, dates, and vanilla until everything is chopped well and the mixture begins to stick together. Add the cherries and pulse just until well incorporated.

Press into a 6" × 6" inch (15 cm × 15 cm) container. Turn out onto a board and cut into 2-inch (5 cm) squares. Wrap and store in the refrigerator for 1 week or in the freezer for several months.

YIELD: NINE 2-INCH (5 CM) SQUARES

Caramel Apple and Walnut Bowl

Juicy apple chunks with almond butter and dates taste just as sweet and delectable as a caramel apple.

2   **apples, chopped**
¼   **cup (60 g) almond butter**
1   **cup (235 ml) almond or flax milk**
6   **dates, chopped**
2   **tablespoons (15 g) chopped walnuts**
½   **teaspoon vanilla extract**

Divide the apples between two bowls. Divide the almond butter between the bowls. Pour the milk in each one and sprinkle the dates, walnuts, and vanilla on top.

YIELD: 2 SERVINGS

Plum Pie

There's no reason not to have pie for breakfast when it's made of healthy raw fruits and nuts. Plum Pie goes really well with Banana ice cream (see recipe page 146) and a little bit of blackberry puree. To make blackberry puree, blend together equal parts blackberries and agave until very smooth and strain through a mesh strainer to remove the seeds.

- ½   **cup (75 g) almonds**
- ½   **cup (90 g) dates**
- 4   **plums, thinly sliced**
- 3   **tablespoons (45 ml) coconut oil**
- 3   **tablespoons (45 ml) agave**

In a food processor fitted with an "S" blade, process the almonds and dates until they're well chopped and begin sticking together.

Press the mixture into the bottom of a 6-inch (15 cm) plate, pie plate, or tart pan. Place in the refrigerator for a few minutes to chill.

In the food processor, again fitted with an "S" blade, process one plum and the oil and agave. Once pureed, spread this evenly over the pie crust. Arrange the remaining plum slices on top of the puree.

YIELD: 2 TO 3 SERVINGS

Nutrition FYI: Plums
Just one average-sized plum has 16 mg vitamin C, 11 mg vitamin K, 259 mg potassium, 27 mg phosphorus, and 12 mg magnesium.

chapter

9

"If you have nothing but love for your avocados, and you find joy in turning them into guacamole, all you need is someone to share it with."

—Jason Mraz, singer-songwriter

Main Dishes

Main dishes are expected to fill you up. They're usually hearty and substantial, and they will stay with you. They are generally more complex than other dishes, as well, and they may take a little more time to prepare.

Traditionally, main dishes have some kind of meat as the primary ingredient, but there are many healthy alternatives that are delicious and will fill you up without bogging you down.

Raw food main dishes can often rely the most on pretending to be favorite cooked food dishes, and many are quite convincing. Nuts and mushrooms can be combined with spices to make savory meat-like dishes such as meat loafs, burgers, and tacos. Old favorites like lasagna can be convincingly created from not much more than zucchini and tomatoes.

Be flexible with what you consider a main dish. While recipes that are specifically intended to be the primary dish are delicious and interesting, a large salad with some luscious avocado and a fantastic dressing can be a perfectly satisfying yet simple dinner.

Nutrition FYI: Bell Peppers

Maximize the nutrition content in bell peppers by letting them ripen, when the vitamin C and cartotenoids will be highest. Eat them raw, too. Bell peppers contain luteolin, which is a flavonoid that's destroyed by heat.

Stuffed Peppers

This is a sweet and savory dish that can be dehydrated to warm it and intensify the flavors.

- 3 tablespoons (45 ml) balsamic vinegar
- 3 tablespoons (45 ml) agave
- 3 tablespoons (45 ml) olive oil
- 1 teaspoon fresh garlic, minced
- ½ teaspoon salt
- ½ teaspoon black pepper
- 10 ounces (280 g) sliced button mushrooms
- 1 cup (175 g) chopped mango
- ¼ cup (40 g) chopped red onion
- 2 red peppers, halved and seeded
  Red-pepper flakes, to taste

In a medium bowl, whisk together the vinegar, agave, oil, garlic, salt, and pepper. Stir in the mushrooms, mango, and onion. Spoon into the red pepper halves and sprinkle a little bit of red-pepper flakes on top.

Dehydrator option: To intensify the flavors and warm the meal, place the stuffed peppers in a 118°F (48°C) dehydrator for an hour or two before serving.

YIELD: 4 STUFFED PEPPER HALVES

Stuffed Avocados

These stuffed avocados are substantial enough to be a light meal and also provide plenty of healthy fats, along with vitamin C.

- 2 ripe avocados
- 3 tablespoons (45 ml) lime juice
- 1 tablespoon (15 ml) agave
- 3 tablespoons (45 ml) olive oil
- 1 teaspoon minced fresh garlic
- ½ teaspoon salt
- ½ teaspoon black pepper
- 1 large tomato
- 3 tablespoons (30 g) chopped red onion
- 3 tablespoons (30 g) chopped green bell pepper
- 2 tablespoons (2 g) chopped fresh cilantro
- 1 jalapeño pepper, chopped

Slice the avocados in half and remove the pits.

In a small bowl, whisk together the lime juice, agave, oil, garlic, salt, and black pepper. Add the tomato, onion, green pepper, cilantro, and jalapeño, and stir well to combine. Spoon the mixture into the seed cavity of each of the four avocado halves.

YIELD: 4 STUFFED AVOCADO HALVES

Easy Lasagna

This is a new but simple twist on an old favorite. Heirloom and Roma (plum) tomatoes work beautifully in this dish and add lovely color, but any tomatoes can be used.

For the Tomato Sauce

1½ cups (270 g) seeded and chopped Roma tomatoes

4 dates, soaked in water for ½ hour

1 teaspoon minced fresh garlic

3 tablespoons (45 ml) olive oil

1 tablespoon (3 g) fresh chopped basil
or ½ teaspoon dried basil

½ teaspoon dried oregano

½ teaspoon salt

½ teaspoon black pepper

For the Almond Ricotta

1 cup (145 g) almonds, soaked overnight

2 tablespoons (30 ml) lemon juice

1 teaspoon minced fresh garlic

1 tablespoon (3 g) fresh chopped basil

½ teaspoon dried oregano

1 teaspoon salt

For the Lasagna

2 cups (240 g) zucchini strips

3 tomatoes, thinly sliced

½ cup (80 g) thinly sliced red onion

½ cup (75 g) chopped green bell pepper

½ cup (8 g) chopped fresh basil leaves

½ cup (8 g) chopped arugula leaves

Salt, to taste

Black pepper, to taste

If you make the tomato sauce and almond ricotta before assembling the lasagna, this becomes an easy and quick project.

To make the tomato sauce: Puree all ingredients in a small blender until very smooth. Set aside.

To make the almond ricotta: Separately puree all ingredients in a small blender until very smooth. This will take a few minutes. Set aside.

To make the lasagna: Place a layer of zucchini strips in the bottom of a 6- to 8-inch (15 to 20 cm) square plate or pan. Add a few spoons of tomato sauce on top of the zucchini strips and spread evenly.

Add a few spoons of the almond ricotta and spread evenly. Layer in a few of the tomato slices, onion slices, and green pepper. Add a few tablespoons (3 g each) of basil and a few tablespoons (3 g each) of arugula. On top of this, make another layer of zucchini strips and continue layering until your ingredients are used. End with a zucchini layer and top with a spoonful of tomato sauce and one of almond ricotta. Add salt and pepper to taste.

YIELD: 2 SERVINGS

Nutrition FYI: Tomatoes
One medium tomato contains about 15 milligrams, or 26 percent, of the daily requirement of vitamin C.

Celery Root Pilaf Recipe

By Jinjee Talifero

Celery root, also known as celeriac, is a root vegetable that tastes similar to celery. It makes a tasty pilaf!

1 medium celery root (look for this in your produce section, it looks like a gnarled root vegetable)

1 teaspoon olive oil or flaxseed oil

½ lemon, juiced

½ teaspoon fresh thyme, minced

Dash or two onion or garlic powder

Salt, to taste

½ avocado and/or tomato

Peel the rough outer skin off the celery root with a kitchen knife, and cut into large chunks. Process in a food processor to fine couscous-size bits.

Add the oil, lemon juice, thyme, onion or garlic powder, and salt, and stir. Add in the avocado. Stir and serve.

YIELD: 1 SERVING

Jinjee Talifero: The Garden Diet is a balanced fresh-foods raw vegan menu plan created by Storm and Jinjee Talifero. The recipes were designed for their five children for great taste, ease of preparation, and optimum nutrition. The Garden Diet's 28 Days Raw and 21 Day Cleanse menu plans have helped hundreds of people to go raw safely and easily! Learn more about Jinjee and her family at http://TheGardenDiet.com.

Lettuce Wraps

These lettuce wraps are filled with healthy deliciousness and are surprisingly hearty and filling. Set up a "wrap bar" with a selection of prepared ingredients, and let everyone make their own.

½ cup Thousand Island Dressing (See recipe on page 75.)

1 cup (145 g) sliced avocado

1 cup (110 g) grated carrot

½ cup (110 g) grated beets

½ cup (80 g) sliced onions

½ cup (35 g) sliced mushrooms

1 cup (45 g) sunflower seed sprouts (See how-to on page 40.)

8 large Romaine lettuce leaves

Place a bit of the avocado, carrot, beets, onion, mushrooms, and sprouts in each Romaine leaf. Finally, drizzle the filling of each wrap with a spoonful or two of dressing.

YIELD: 8 WRAPS

Raw Farmers' Market Eggplant Tacos

By Beth Mickens

Thin slices of eggplant act as taco shells in this "rawfully" delightful main dish that's a little elaborate, but still remarkably easy to prepare!

For the Eggplant "Tortillas"

1	large, round purple eggplant
1	teaspoon salt

For the Mixed Seasoned Veggie "Saute"

¼	cup (40 g) chopped red bell pepper
¼	cup (30 g) chopped zucchini
¼	cup (30 g) raw corn kernels
¼	cup (45 g) quartered cherry tomatoes
2	tablespoons (12 g) sliced scallions
1	tablespoon (1 g) chopped fresh cilantro
1	tablespoon (15 ml) lime juice
¼	teaspoon chili powder
¼	teaspoon cumin powder
	Pinch of salt
	Pinch of red-pepper flakes (optional)

For the Guacamole

1	avocado, skin and pit removed
¼	cup (40 g) chopped red onion
1	jalapeño pepper, chopped (optional)
⅛	teaspoon grated garlic
1	tablespoon (1 g) cilantro
1	tablespoon (15 ml) lime juice
	Salt, to taste

For the Creamy Sweet Chipotle Lime Sauce

¼	cup (35 g) raw, shelled hemp seeds or other nut, or 2 tablespoons (32 g) raw nut butter
2	tablespoons (30 ml) lime juice
2	tablespoons (30 ml) water
2 to 3	teaspoons maple syrup
1	teaspoon chipotle powder
	Salt, to taste
	Sprouts, for garnish

To make the eggplant tortillas: Slice the eggplant widthwise into slices approximately ⅛- to ¼-inch (3-to-6 mm) thick. Place the slices into a colander and add the salt. Toss to combine, and allow to sit over a bowl or the sink for about 30 minutes, or until they have released water and are soft and pliable.

To make the sauté: In a small bowl, combine the bell pepper, zucchini, corn, tomatoes, scallions, cilantro, lime juice, chili powder, cumin, and salt. Add red-pepper flakes to taste, if using. Toss to combine and set aside.

To make the guacamole: In a bowl, mash together the avocado, onion, jalapeño, if using, garlic, cilantro, and lime juice. Salt to taste and set aside.

To make the sauce: In a blender, add the hemp seeds, lime juice, water, maple syrup, chipotle powder, and salt to taste. Blend until well blended and creamy. Set aside.

Once the eggplant slices are finished sweating, rinse well with cold water and pat dry, gently squeezing out any excess water.

To assemble the tacos: For each eggplant "tortilla," spread a thin layer of guacamole, fill with 1 to 2 tablespoons (TK) of sautéed veggies, top with sprouts, and drizzle with the creamy, chipotle lime sauce. Fold over and serve.

YIELD: 6 TO 8 TACOS

Beth Mickens is a working mom from Gainesville, VA, who enjoys using her spare time to prepare raw foods to share with her blog audience at the Split Plate. Beth started her vegan journey a little more than five years ago, transitioning to a raw food diet four years later, and loves the benefits a raw food lifestyle has to offer: an overabundance of energy, life, joy, and fulfillment. To learn more about Beth and to see some of her recipes, visit her at TheSplitPlate.blogspot.com.

Cucumber Boats with Mango

Spicy mango fills these cucumber cups for an easy-to-make, light, and refreshing dish.

- 1½ cups (265 g) chopped mango
- ¼ cup (40 g) minced onion
- ¼ cup (40 g) chopped red bell pepper
- 1 tablespoon finely minced jalapeño pepper
- 3 tablespoons (45 ml) olive oil
- 3 tablespoons (45 ml) agave
- 3 tablespoons (45 ml) apple cider vinegar
- ½ teaspoon salt plus more to taste
- ½ teaspoon black pepper plus more to taste
- 2 large cucumbers
- 1 tablespoon (6 g) chopped fresh mint leaves (optional)
- 1 teaspoon crushed red-pepper flakes (optional)

In a medium bowl, mix the mango with the onion, red bell pepper, and jalapeño.

In a small cup, whisk together the oil, agave, vinegar, salt, and pepper, and pour over the mango mix. Stir to coat.

Slice the cucumbers in half lengthwise, and scoop out the seed cavities. Fill each cavity with the mango mixture. Add more salt and pepper to taste and mint leaves and red-pepper flakes, if using.

The cucumber boats are best served fresh, but can be stored in a lidded container in the refrigerator for a day or two.

YIELD: 4 SERVINGS

Cucumber Noodles with Creamy Dill Sauce

Cucumber and dill is a classic combination, and this dish is light, summery, and fresh.

- ⅔ cup (95 g) cashews, soaked for 30 minsutes and drained
- ⅔ cup (155 ml) water, for blending
- 3 tablespoons (45 ml) lemon juice
- 1 tablespoon (10 g) chopped onion
- 1 teaspoon agave
- 1 teaspoon dried dill
- 1 large clove garlic or 1 teaspoon minced garlic
- ½ teaspoon salt
- 2 cucumbers

In a blender, puree the cashews, water, lemon juice, onion, agave, dill, garlic, and salt until very creamy and smooth.

Cut the cucumbers into strips (noodles) using a vegetable spiralizer or a knife and vegetable peeler. Add the sauce to the cucumber noodles.

YIELD: 2 SERVINGS

Nutrition FYI: Dill

The volatile oils in dill are chemoprotective, which means they can help neutralize carcinogens, such as those found in cigarette smoke and grilled foods.

Tomato and Watermelon Layered Dish

Tomato and watermelon are perfect partners in this easy and refreshing dish that is ideal for a hot summer day. Best of all, it only takes minutes to prepare.

- ¼ **cup (60 ml) olive oil**
- ¼ **cup (60 ml) agave**
- ¼ **cup (60 ml) balsamic vinegar**
- ½ **teaspoon salt**
- ½ **teaspoon black pepper**
- 1 **teaspoon minced fresh garlic**
- 2 **cups (300 g) thinly sliced watermelon, rinds removed**
- 2 **cups (360 g) thinly sliced tomatoes**
- ½ **cup (75 g) sliced green bell pepper**
- ½ **cup (50 g) sliced scallions**

In a bowl, whisk together the oil, agave, vinegar, salt, black pepper, and garlic.

Assemble the watermelon, tomatoes, bell pepper, and scallions in layers, much like putting together a dish of lasagna. Lay down the first layer of watermelon. Then add a layer of tomato, then a layer of bell pepper and onion. Spoon some of the dressing onto each layer. Continue making layers until the ingredients have been used up.

This dish is best fresh, but any leftovers can be stored in the refrigerator for a day or two.

YIELD: 2 SERVINGS

Tomato Sandwiches on Easy Carrot Bread

These tomato sandwiches can be served with any raw soup or chili for a fantastic lunch or filling dinner.

For the Carrot Bread
- 1 **cup (110 g) grated carrots**
- 1 **cup (100 g) ground flaxseeds**
- ¼ **cup (60 ml) olive oil**
- ¾ **cup (175 ml) water**
- ½ **teaspoon salt**

For the Filling
- 1 **tomato, sliced**
- 1 **small onion, sliced**
- 6 **lettuce leaves**
- ¼ **cup mayo (60 g)**
- **Salt, to taste**

To make the bread: Place all the bread ingredients into a medium bowl and stir to combine well. Let rest for 15 minutes so the flaxseeds can soak up the moisture. Then spread the dough onto a lined dehydrator sheet in a square about ¼-inch (6-mm) thick. Dehydrate for 3 hours at 118°F (48°C) and then peel from the dehydrator sheet and flip over onto an unlined dehydrator tray. Continue drying for another 3 hours, until the bread is a little crispy but still pliable.

Assemble the sandwiches by cutting the bread into 6 equal rectangular pieces. Then layer on the tomato, onion, and lettuce leaves. Add a dollop of mayo and salt to taste.

These sandwiches are best served right away but can be stored tightly wrapped in the refrigerator for up to a few days.

YIELD: 3 SANDWICHES

Cherry BBQ Sauce

By Andrea Wycoff, a.k.a. Betty Rawker

This is really yummy over fruit and veggie skewers, with the cantaloupe being everyone's favorite.

- 2 cups (310 g) dark sweet cherries (fresh or frozen and defrosted, pits removed)
- 2 tablespoons (30 ml) blackberry vinegar or apple cider vinegar
- 1 tablespoon (45 ml) coconut aminos or tamari
- 1 tablespoon (10 g) minced dried onion or 1 teaspoon onion powder
- 2 tablespoons (30 ml) maple syrup
- 1 tablespoon (15 ml) black strap molasses (It's not raw, but it adds great BBQ flavor.)
- ½ teaspoon raw mustard
- ¼ teaspoon chipotle powder
- 1 clove garlic
- 1 teaspoon fresh ginger
- ½ teaspoon black pepper
- ½ teaspoon sea salt

Blend all ingredients in a high-speed blender. Serve with fresh or dehydrated veggies, or use in place of regular BBQ sauce when grilling. This stuff is absolutely amazing when served cooked or raw!

YIELD: 2½ CUPS (630 G)

Andrea Wyckoff chose to name her little business "Betty Rawker" (a fun play on Betty Crocker) because she's a total foodie who has fallen head over heels in love with raw foods! She strives to create comfort foods that are truly nourishing for our bodies! Eating pure and raw has increased her overall energy, re-awakened her spirit, and provided the ultimate creative outlet! To learn more about Andrea/"Betty Rawker" and to see some of her recipes, visit her at http://www.bettyrawker.com.

Marinated "Grilled" Veggies

Serve with a side or drizzle of fresh Cherry BBQ Sauce. (recipe at left) Enjoy!

- ½ cup (80 g) cubed cantaloupe
- ½ cup (75 g) chopped red bell pepper
- ½ cup (80 g) chopped red onion
- ½ cup (85 g) chopped peaches
- ½ cup (60 g) chopped zucchini
- ½ cup (90 g) cherry tomato halves
- 1 lemon, juiced
- 2 tablespoons (30 ml) olive oil
- 2 pinches of sea salt
- 1 cup Cherry BBQ Sauce

In a large bowl, combine the fruit and veggies.

In a small bowl, mix together the lemon juice, oil, and salt.

Pour the marinade into the large bowl, and hand toss the fruits and veggies. Carefully stick the chunks of fruit and veggies onto 8 wooden skewers.

Lay skewers on a dehydrator tray, and dehydrate at 115ºF (46ºC) for 2 hours. Apply Cherry BBQ Sauce, and dehydrate for another 1 to 2 hours. (The fruit and veggies will take on a "grilled" look yet still be full of "rawsome" flavor.)

YIELD: 3 CUPS (750 G)

Nutrition FYI: Cherries

Cherries are high in pectin, which is a soluble fiber that reduces "bad" cholesterol. They also contain nineteen times the beta-carotene that is found in blueberries.

Yellow Squash Ribbons with Arugula Pesto

Arugula makes a peppery and slightly spicy pesto that is an interesting change of pace.

- 1 cup (20 g) arugula leaves
- ½ cup (60 ml) olive oil
- 1 clove garlic
- ¼ cup (35 g) pine nuts, plus additional for topping
- ½ teaspoon salt
- 2 tablespoons (20 g) nutritional yeast
- 1 yellow summer squash or any summer squash

In a blender, puree the arugula leaves, oil, garlic, pine nuts, salt, and nutritional yeast until smooth.

Shave the squash into ribbons, or use the wide ribbon blade on a vegetable spiralizer. Assemble the squash ribbons on a plate, and drizzle with the arugula pesto. Top with pine nuts.

Leftover pesto can be stored, covered, in the refrigerator for up to 3 days.

YIELD: 2 SERVINGS

Beet Strands with Basil Nut Cream

Beets are quite hearty, and the nut cream is substantial. The combination makes this a dish that will really fill you up.

- ⅔ cup (95 g) cashews, soaked for a few hours and drained
- ⅔ cup (155 ml) water
- 3 tablespoons (3 g) chopped fresh basil or 1 tablespoon dried basil
- 1 large clove garlic or 1 teaspoon minced
- ½ teaspoon salt
- ½ teaspoon black pepper
- 2 or 3 beets
  Cherry tomatoes, for topping

In a blender, puree the cashews, water, basil, garlic, salt, and pepper until very smooth.

Cut the beets into thin strands using a vegetable spiralizer or a knife and vegetable peeler. Add the cream to the beet strands. Top with the cherry tomatoes.

YIELD: 2 SERVINGS

Nutrition FYI: Arugula

Arugula is a great source of folic acid and vitamins A, C, and K as well as minerals, such as iron and copper. It also has a long tradition as an aphrodisiac!

Nutrition FYI: Beets

Beets contain betalains, which are unique phytonutrients and include betanin and vulgaxanthin. Both are anti-inflammatory and antioxidants. They also provide detox support. The betelains in beets are quite sensitive to heat and degrade under higher temperatures, so raw sources are best.

Stroodles (Apple Strudel Noodles)

More like a delightful dessert than a main dish, this sweet apple treat adds walnuts for extra nutrition and healthy fats.

3	large apples
¼	cup (60 ml) agave
3	tablespoons (45 ml) lemon juice
3	tablespoons (45 ml) olive oil
1	teaspoon ground cinnamon
½	teaspoon ground nutmeg
½	teaspoon salt
¼	cup (30 g) chopped walnuts

If they're not organic, peel the apples. If they're organic, leave the skins on if you like. Core the apples using an apple corer or a sharp knife. Then use the spiralizer to cut them into strips (noodles) using the thin blade. Alternatively, use a sharp knife and vegetable peeler to make the noodles. (See how-to on page 43.)

In a bowl, whisk together the remaining ingredients, except for the walnuts, and pour over the apple noodles. Stir well to coat. Toss the chopped walnuts on the top just before serving.

YIELD: 2 SERVINGS

Nutrition FYI: Cinnamon

Cinnamon has been shown to regulate blood sugar, reduce bad cholesterol, fight infections, reduce the pain of arthritis, and slow the growth of cancer, and it also acts as a natural food preservative. This warm and wonderful herb also contains fiber, calcium, iron, and manganese.

Pad Thai

Traditionally, Pad Thai is a dish made of fried white noodles and vegetables. This recipe uses zucchini noodles and fresh ingredients for a healthier version.

3	cups (750 g) zucchini noodles
1	cup (110 g) grated carrots
½	cup (45 g) grated purple cabbage
½	cup (75 g) thinly sliced red bell pepper
6	scallions, sliced
1	cup (50 g) mung bean sprouts
½	cup (130 g) almond butter
1	cup (235 ml) orange juice
3	tablespoons (45 ml) agave
1	tablespoon (8 g) fresh grated ginger or 1 teaspoon dried
1	tablespoon (15 ml) soy sauce
½ to 1	teaspoon cayenne pepper
½ to 1	teaspoon salt

Arrange the zucchini noodles on two plates. Sprinkle the carrots, cabbage, bell pepper, two and bean sprouts over the top.

In a bowl, whisk together the almond butter, orange juice, agave, ginger, soy sauce, cayenne pepper, and salt. Taste for salt and cayenne, and adjust to taste. Then pour the sauce over the vegetables and noodles.

Pad Thai is best served fresh, but leftovers can be stored in the refrigerator for a day or two.

YIELD: ABOUT 2½ CUPS (625 G)

Zucchini Linguine with Cheesy Red Bell Pepper Sauce and Spinach Basil Pesto

Elegant but easy, this linguine is substantial enough to satisfy even the hungriest diner.

For the Sauce

- 1 cup (145 g) cashews, soaked for 30 minutes and drained
- 1 cup (150 g) sliced red bell pepper
- 3 tablespoons (30 g) nutritional yeast
- 1 teaspoon minced fresh garlic
- 1 tablespoon (15 ml) lemon juice
- 1 tablespoon (15 ml) soy sauce
- 1 cup (235 ml) water
- ½ teaspoon salt

For the Pesto

- 1 cup (30 g) chopped fresh spinach
- 1 cup (40 g) chopped fresh basil
- ½ cup (120 ml) olive oil
- ¼ cup (35 g) pine nuts
- ½ teaspoon salt
- ½ teaspoon black pepper

For assembling

- 3 cups (750 g) zucchini noodles

To make the sauce: Place all sauce ingredients a blender. Process on high until the sauce is smooth and creamy. (This may take a minute or two.)

To make the pesto: Place all pesto ingredients in a blender and process on high speed until smooth.

On a plate, make a bed of the noodles, then add the sauce and the pesto. Add more salt and pepper to taste, if needed.

YIELD: ABOUT 2 SERVINGS

Nutritional FYI: Red Bell Peppers
Red bell peppers contain almost three times the recommended daily allowance for vitamin C, as well as significant amounts of vitamins A and B_6, and fiber.

Pizza

This traditional treat gets a healthy spin with fresh, raw, plant-based ingredients. You'll never miss the old stuff!

For the Crust

- ½ cup (84 g) flaxseeds, finely ground
- ½ cup (75 g) almonds, finely ground
- ½ cup (50 g) chia seeds, finely ground
- 1 ½ teaspoons dried basil
- 1 ½ teaspoons dried oregano
- ¼ teaspoon thyme
- ½ teaspoon salt
- 2 tablespoons (30 ml) olive oil
- ½ cup (120 ml) water, more or less for mixing

For the Cheese

- ½ cup (75 g) cashews, soaked for 30 minutes and drained
- ¼ cup (60 ml) water
- 3 tablespoons (30 g) nutritional yeast
- 2 tablespoons (30 ml) lemon juice
- 1 teaspoon minced fresh garlic
- 1 teaspoon salt

For the Tomato Sauce

- 1 ripe tomato
- ½ cup (30 g) sun-dried tomatoes, softened in water for 30 minutes and drained
- 1 tablespoon (15 ml) agave
- 1 teaspoon dried basil
- 1 teaspoon dried oregano
- ½ cup (120 ml) water more or less for blending
- ½ teaspoon salt

For the Toppings

- ½ cup (35 g) mushrooms
- ½ cup (45 g) halved cherry tomatoes
- 4 scallions, sliced thinly
- 1 cup (145 g) avocado slices
- ½ cup (10 g) chopped arugula

To make the crust: A day ahead of time, grind the flaxseeds, almonds, and chia seeds using a spice or coffee grinder. Place them in a large bowl, and add the basil, oregano, and salt. Stir to combine the dry ingredients.

Add the oil and water and mix well until a dough forms. Let the dough rest in the bowl for 15 minutes to allow the flax and chia to soak up the moisture and become gelatinous. Divide into 4 crusts, and spread the dough out on lined dehydrator sheets in ¼-inch-thick (6 mm) rounds. Dry for 4 hours at 118°F (48°C). Then, remove the crusts from the dehydrator, and flip onto an unlined dehydrator tray. Dry for 4 more hours, or until the crusts are quite dry and almost crispy.

To make the cheese: Place all cheese ingredients in a blender and process on high speed until the cheese is smooth and creamy. (This will take a minute or two. A small bullet type blender works well for this.)

To make the tomato sauce: Place all tomato sauce ingredients in a blender and process on high until the sauce is smooth.

Prepare the topping ingredients, and assemble the pizzas. On each of the crusts, spread a quarter of the tomato sauce. Then spread a layer of cheese sauce over the tomato sauce on each crust. Finally, add the toppings of your choice.

These can be eaten just like this, or placed back in the dehydrator for 1½ hour at 118°F (48°C) to warm.

Pizzas are best served right away but can be stored in a lidded container in the refrigerator for a day or two. The crusts can be made in bulk in advance and stored tightly wrapped in the freezer until ready to use for up to several months.

YIELD: 4 PIZZAS

Pizza Trivia

Historically, pizza did not include tomatoes until the sixteenth century. At that time, tomatoes were abundant, and the people of Naples were poor. So, the classic partnership was born of necessity. It's also believed that Persian soldiers were making something very much like pizza in the sixth century BCE.

Pizza-Stuffed Mushrooms

The sauce is spicy, and the Portobellos are succulent in this delicious and hearty dish.

For the Cheese Sauce

- ½ **cup (75 g) cashews**
- ½ **cup (120 ml) water**
- 1 **tablespoon (15 ml) lemon juice**
- 2 **tablespoons (20 g) nutritional yeast**
- 1 **teaspoon salt**

For the Tomato Sauce

- 1 **ripe tomato**
- ½ **cup (40 g) sun-dried tomatoes, softened in water for 30 minutes and drained**
- 1 **tablespoon (15 ml) agave**
- 1 **teaspoon dried basil**
- 1 **teaspoon dried oregano**
- ½ **cup (120 ml) water, more or less for blending**
- ½ **teaspoon salt**

For assembling

- 4 **Portobello mushrooms**

To make the cheese sauce: Place all cheese sauce ingredients in a blender and process on high speed until the sauce is smooth and creamy. (This will take a minute or two.)

To make the tomato sauce: Place all the tomato sauce ingredients in a blender and process until smooth. (This will take a minute or two.)

Place the mushrooms with the underside up on a lined dehydrator tray. Spread about 2 to 3 tablespoons (30 to 45 ml) of tomato sauce in the center of each. Spread a dollop of cheese sauce over the tomato sauce.

Place the Portobellos into the dehydrator, and at 118°F (48°C) for about an hour. (This will warm the mushrooms and intensify the flavors.)

These pizza-stuffed mushrooms are best served immediately, but can be refrigerated in a container for a day or two.

YIELD: 4 PORTOBELLO PIZZAS

Variation: Instead of Portobellos, use a pound of button mushrooms with stems removed for bite-size pizza treats.

Walnut Apple and Sprouted Lentil Loaf with BBQ Sauce

This lentil loaf is meaty, hearty, and robust. The BBQ sauce is sweet and spicy. Together, they make a perfect and filling pair.

1   cup (100 g) walnuts, coarsely ground
¼   cup (28 g) ground flaxseeds
½   teaspoon thyme
½   teaspoon sage
½   teaspoon dried oregano
¾   teaspoon salt
½   teaspoon black pepper
½   cup (55 g) grated carrot
¼   cup (40 g) finely chopped onion
1   cup (50 g) sprouted lentils
     (See how-to on page 42.)
¼   cup (40 g) chopped apple
½   cup (115 g) apple puree
     BBQ Sauce (See recipe on page 129.)

Place the walnuts, flaxseeds, thyme, sage, oregano, salt, and pepper in a food processor fitted with an "S" blade. Pulse until they are well mixed.

Add in the carrot, onion, and lentils, and pulse several times until the lentils are coarsely chopped and everything is mixed well.

Add in the apple and apple puree last, pulsing again until everything is well mixed and is beginning to stick together. Set aside, and let the mix rest for about 15 minutes.

Divide the mix into four equal parts and form into rectangular loaves shapes on lined dehydrator sheets. Make the loafs about ¾-inch (2 cm) thick. Dry at 118°F (48°C) for 3 hours, until the loaves are warmed and starting to get dry and crispy on the outside.

Spread 2 to 3 tablespoons (30 to 45 ml) BBQ sauce on the top of each loaf, and dehydrate for 1 more hour at 118°F (48°C). The loaf will be warmed, a little crisp on the outside, and the BBQ sauce will be more concentrated.

Serve immediately, straight from the dehydrator. Leftovers can be stored in a lidded container in the refrigerator for up to 3 days.

YIELD: 4 LENTIL LOAVES

Variation: Walnut Apple Lentil Burgers

Make the lentil loaf mix as directed in the recipe above. Shape the walnut lentil loaf mix into burger shapes, and dehydrate at 118°F (48°C) for about 4 hours, until crispy on the outside and soft on the inside. Serve on a bed of lettuce with mustard and ketchup. (See recipes on page 129.)

Chili

This looks like a lot of ingredients, but it's a simple recipe. Spicy and flavorful, this chili is also hearty enough to keep you feeling well-fed. It's perfect for a chilly fall day, especially when warmed.

- ½ cup (90 g) chopped tomatoes
- ½ cup (40 g) sun-dried tomatoes, soaked for 30 minutes and drained
- 1 teaspoon fresh minced garlic
- 1½ teaspoons chili powder
- 1 teaspoon ground cumin
- ½ teaspoon dried oregano
- ½ teaspoon dried thyme
- 3 tablespoons (45 ml) agave
- 1 teaspoon salt
- ½ teaspoon black pepper
- 1½ cups (355 ml) water
- 1 cup (100 g) sprouted lentils (See how-to on page 42.)
- ¼ cup (40 g) chopped onion
- ½ cup (55 g) grated carrot
- ½ cup (35 g) chopped mushrooms
- ¼ cup (30 g) finely chopped celery
- ¼ cup (40 g) chopped green bell pepper
- 1 chopped jalapeño pepper, with seeds and ribs removed
- 1 cup (180 g) chopped tomatoes

Place the tomatoes, sun-dried tomatoes, garlic, chili powder, cumin, oregano, thyme, agave, salt, pepper, and water into a food processor fitted with an "S" blade. Pulse a few times to get the ingredients mixed, then process on high speed until the sauce is very smooth. (This will take a minute or two.)

Into the sauce, add the lentils, onion, carrot, mushrooms, celery, bell pepper, and jalapeño. Pulse several times to make sure everything is chopped and well mixed. Finally, add the tomatoes and pulse once or twice.

To warm the chili, place in a wide, shallow bowl in a dehydrator set to 118°F (48°C) for about 1 hour. Alternatively, this chili can be very gently heated in a warm pan on the stove, though be careful not to let it get too hot.

Leftover chili can be stored in a lidded container in the refrigerator for up to 3 days. Warm before serving again.

YIELD: ABOUT 6 CUPS (1500 G)

Nutritional FYI: Chili Peppers

Chili peppers are amazingly nutritious. Just 100 grams contain 32 percent of your recommended daily amount of vitamin A, 39 percent of vitamin B6, 240 percent of vitamin C, 13 percent of iron, 14 percent of copper, 7 percent of potassium, and has *no* cholesterol.

Taco Salad in a Jar

This is a convenient and easy way to take a delicious raw meal on the go. Taco salad in a jar will travel easily to work or school. Four 24-ounce (710 ml) lidded glass jars are required for this salad.

For the Taco Filling

- ½   cup (60 g) chopped walnuts
- ½   cup (50 g) sprouted lentils (See how-to on page 42.)
- ½   teaspoon garlic powder
- ½   teaspoon onion powder
- ½   teaspoon ground paprika
- ½   teaspoon chili powder
- ½   teaspoon cumin
- ½   teaspoon salt
- ½   teaspoon black pepper
- 2   tablespoons (30 ml) olive oil
- 3   tablespoons (45 ml) water

For the Salad Layers

- 2   cups (360 g) chopped tomatoes
- ½   cup (80 g) chopped red onion
- 1   jalapeño pepper, finely chopped
- ½   cup (50 g) raw corn kernels, optional
- 1   cup (145 g) sliced avocado
- 6   cups (330 g) chopped Romaine lettuce
-     Salt, to taste
-     Black pepper, to taste

To make the taco filling: In a medium bowl, combine all of the taco filling ingredients and mix well.

To make the layers: Divide the tomatoes, onion, jalapeño, corn, and avocado between the four jars, and layer them in the bottom of the jar in the order that they're listed.

Divide the taco filling between the four jars, and place on top of the avocado slices.

Divide the lettuce between the four jars, and place on top of the taco filling.

To serve, pour the salad out onto a large serving plate or bowl, and add salt and pepper to taste.

Taco salad in a jar can be stored in the refrigerator for up to 3 days.

YIELD: 4 JARS

chapter

10

"All sorrows are less with bread.**"**

—Miguel de Cervantes, Spanish novelist, poet, and playwright

Crackers, Chips & Breads

Having crunchy snacks on hand can make a raw life easier and more enjoyable. Common ingredients in raw crackers include flax, which is high in magnesium, phosphorus, and copper, and buckwheat, which lowers the risk of diabetes. And raw crackers and breads are free of the unhealthy ingredients found in most commercial crackers, such as processed wheat and grains, corn syrup, trans fat, and high levels of sodium. It's increasingly common to find a variety of raw chips and crackers ready-made in stores, and these can be wonderfully convenient treats. However, making your own will almost always be the better bargain, and the freshness factor can't be beat.

Kale chips are also represented in this chapter, and they're super-easy to make and taste great. They're also endlessly adaptable and can be flavored in a myriad of ways. Kale is full of vitamin K, which is essential for heart and bone health, as well as vitamins A and C, manganese, and fiber.

Kale is also well-known for lowering the risk of several cancers, its anti-inflammatory properties, and protecting vision. Nutritional yeast adds a deliciously cheesy taste to crackers and chips and provides a tremendous amount of B vitamins. Just 3 tablespoons (30 g) adds more than 800 percent of the recommended daily requirement for B_1, 700 percent of B_2, 350 percent of B_3, 550 percent of B_6, and 310 percent of folic acid.

A dehydrator will definitely come in handy when making raw crackers, and it's really best to use one. It makes the process convenient and will yield the finest result, but it's not absolutely essential. If you don't have a dehydrator, an oven with the door left ajar and set on the lowest temperature can be used instead.

Store crackers and breads at room temperature in a lidded container. Place them in a dehydrator for ½ hour before serving to warm them and ensure they're crispy.

Basic Flax Crackers

Flax crackers are easy to make and are an excellent snack. Great on their own, and a raw food standby, they go particularly well with any salsa as well as raw cheeses.

1½   cups (150 g) ground flaxseeds
½   cup (84 g) whole flaxseeds
1½   cups (355 ml) water, or more for mixing
1   teaspoon salt

In a bowl, combine all ingredients, and mix until a sticky dough forms. Spread the dough out on a lined dehydrator tray about ⅛-inch (3 mm) thick. Using a sharp knife, score the dough in 1- or 2-inch (2.5- to 5-cm) squares. Dehydrate at 118°F (48°C) for several hours. Peel away from the tray liner and flip onto an unlined tray. Let dry for another 4 to 5 hours until thoroughly dry. Break at the score lines into square crackers.

Leftover flax crackers can be stored at room temperature in a lidded container for up to a few days. If the crackers lose some of their crispiness, just pop them in the dehydrator for ½ hour.

YIELD: ABOUT 30 CRACKERS

Variations

Here are some ways to vary the Basic Flax Cracker:

- For more intense flavor, add 1 tablespoon (9 g) garlic powder and 1 tablespoon (7 g) onion powder.
- Add 1 tablespoon (9 g) dried oregano, 1 tablespoon (3 g) dried basil, 1 teaspoon garlic powder, and 1 tablespoon (5 g) onion powder for an Italian-flavored flax cracker.
- For a French twist, add 1 tablespoon (2 g) tarragon and ¼ cup (35 g) sesame seeds.
- Add ½ cup (40 g) chopped sundried tomatoes.
- Add 1 tablespoon (2 g) chopped fresh rosemary and 1 teaspoon dried thyme.

Leftover Pulp Crackers

If you make nut and seed milks, there will inevitably be pulp left over. But there's no need to let it go to waste. Flax, almond, cashew, 1 sunflower seed pulp, and more can be used to make a delicious and nutritious cracker.

- 2 cups (220 g) nut or seed pulp or 2 cups (200 g) ground nuts
- 1 cup (100 g) ground flaxseeds
- ½ cup (70 g) sesame seeds
- 1 cup (160 g) finely chopped onion
- ¼ cup (40 g) nutritional yeast
- 1 teaspoon minced fresh garlic
- 1 tablespoon (7 g) onion powder
- 1 teaspoon garlic powder
- 1 teaspoon chopped dried rosemary
- ½ teaspoon sage
- ½ teaspoon thyme
- 1 teaspoon salt
- 1½ cups (355 ml) water, or more for mixing

In a bowl, combine all ingredients, and mix until a thick dough forms. Spread the dough out on a lined dehydrator tray about ⅛-inch (3-mm) thick. Using a sharp knife, score the dough into 2- by 3-inch (5 by 7.5 cm) rectangles.

Dehydrate at 118°F (48°C) for several hours. Peel away from the tray liner and flip onto an unlined tray. Let dry for another 4 to 5 hours until thoroughly dry. Break at the score lines into rectangular crackers.

Store any leftovers at room temperature in a lidded container.

YIELD: ABOUT 48 CRACKERS

Curried Chia-Kraut Crackers

By Judita Wignall

Judita's fantastic crackers use the unexpected ingredient of sauerkraut. Sauerkraut is full of healthy probiotics and adds a great flavor, too. (See sauerkraut how-to on page 49.) You will need to plan ahead by soaking 1 cup (135 g) shelled sunflower seeds for 6 to 8 hours and soaking ½ cup (75 g) almonds for 8 to 12 hours.

2	cups (470 ml) water
⅓	cup (50 g) ground chia seeds
1	cup (135 g) shelled sunflower seeds, soaked and rinsed
½	cup (75 g) almonds, soaked and rinsed
1	cup (120 g) sauerkraut (See how-to on page 49.)
1	small clove garlic, crushed
1½	tablespoons (9 g) curry powder
½	teaspoon garlic powder
½	teaspoon onion powder
1	teaspoon sea salt

In a bowl, combine the water and chia seeds. Mix well and set aside.

Place the sunflower seeds and almonds in a food processor and process until broken down but slightly coarse. Add the sauerkraut and pulse until incorporated.

Transfer the mixture to a large bowl, and add the garlic, curry powder, garlic powder, onion powder, and salt until well mixed. Add the soaked chia and mix very well.

Spread the mixture evenly over a 15- × 15-inch (37.5- × 37.5-cm) dehydrator tray lined with a nonstick sheet.

Dry for 1½ hours at 110°F (43°C), then score into desired-size pieces.

Return to the dehydrator for 6 hours.

Flip the crackers onto a mesh dehydrator tray and dry for another 10 hours, or until dry and crispy. Store in an airtight container.

YIELD: ABOUT 30 CRACKERS

Judita Wignall is a raw food chef, author, a Certified Holistic Health Counselor trained at the Institute for Integrative Nutrition, and a Raw Food Chef and Nutrition Educator from the Living Light Culinary Institute. She's also been a commercial actress and model as well as a singer/songwriter/rocker. She's the author of *Going Raw* and *Raw and Simple*. She and her husband also own the online raw food supply store, City and Sea Trading, Co. rawjudita.com

Scallion and Kale Flat Bread

Perfect with nearly any topping, this savory flat bread is deliciously healthy. My favorite way to enjoy this is with a little bit of a cashew cheese, some caramelized onions (see page 48), and balsamic syrup (see page 131).

- 1   cup (100 g) ground flaxseeds
- 1   cup (120 g) ground buckwheat
- ½   cup (70 g) sesame seeds
- 1   cup (100 g) chopped scallions
- 1   cup (67 g) finely chopped kale
- 1   teaspoon minced fresh garlic
- 1   teaspoon garlic powder
- 1   tablespoon (7 g) onion powder
- 1   tablespoon (3 g) dried oregano
- 1   teaspoon salt

In a bowl, combine all ingredients, and mix until a thick dough forms. Spread the dough out on a lined dehydrator tray about ¼-inch (6-mm) thick. Using a sharp knife, score the dough into 4-inch (10-cm) squares.

Dehydrate at 118°F (48°C) for about 4 hours. Peel away from the tray liner and flip onto an unlined tray, and continue dehydrating for another 2 hours, or until the bread is crispy on the outside and still a little soft on the inside.

YIELD: ABOUT 18 PIECES

Cheesy Spicy Flax Crackers

Make these as hot or not as you like. Add more chipotle and cayenne for more heat or don't add as much to keep the temperature on low. Carrot juice adds a cheesy color, but use water instead if desired.

2	cups (200 g) ground flaxseeds
1	cup (168 g) whole flaxseeds
½	cup (60 g) nutritional yeast
½ to 1	teaspoon chipotle powder
½	teaspoon cayenne pepper, or to taste
1	tablespoon (7 g) onion powder
1	teaspoon garlic powder
½	cup (80 g) finely chopped onion
1	teaspoon salt
1½	cups (355 ml) carrot juice or water, or more for mixing

In a bowl, combine all ingredients, and mix until a thick dough forms. Spread the dough out on a lined dehydrator tray about ⅛-inch (3 mm) thick. Using a sharp knife, score the dough in 1- or 2-inch (2.5- or 5-cm) triangles. Dehydrate at 118°F (48°C) for 5 hours. Peel away from the tray liner and flip onto an unlined tray. Let dry for another 4 to 5 hours until thoroughly dry. Break at the score lines into triangular crackers.

Store any leftovers at room temperature in a lidded container.

YIELD: ABOUT 36 CRACKERS

Corn Chips

These are so much healthier than store-bought corn chips, and they're more delicious, too. Enjoy these tasty chips on their own or with any salsa or soup. Frozen and thawed corn can be used but may not be entirely raw.

2	cups (210 g) corn kernels, fresh or frozen
1	cup (100 g) finely ground flaxseeds
1	tablespoon (9 g) garlic powder
1	tablespoon (7 g) onion powder
½ to 1	teaspoon cayenne pepper
1	teaspoon salt
1½	cups water

Combine all ingredients in a bowl, and mix until a thick dough forms. Spread the dough out on a lined dehydrator tray about ⅛-inch thick. Using a sharp knife, score the dough into 2- × 3-inch (5-cm × 7.5-cm) rectangles or triangles.

Dehydrate at 118°F (48°C) for several hours. Peel away from the tray liner and flip onto an unlined tray. Let dry for another 4 to 5 hours until thoroughly dry. Break at the score lines into rectangular or triangular crackers.

Store any leftovers at room temperature in a lidded container.

YIELD: ABOUT 36 TO 48 CHIPS

Sun-Dried Tomato and Basil Crackers

Sun-dried tomatoes and basil add a delectable Italian flair to these crispy crackers.

- **1 cup (100 g) ground buckwheat**
- **1 cup (100 g) finely ground flaxseeds**
- **½ cup (50 g) finely ground almonds**
- **½ cup (40 g) sun-dried tomatoes, soaked for 1 hour and rinsed**
- **½ cup (50 g) finely chopped scallions**
- **1 tablespoon (2 g) dried basil**
- **2 teaspoons dried oregano**
- **1 teaspoon garlic powder**
- **1 tablepoon (7 g) onion powder**
- **1 teaspoon salt**
- **1 cup (235 ml) water**

In a bowl, combine all ingredients, and mix until a thick dough forms. Spread the dough out on a lined dehydrator tray about ⅛-inch (3-mm) thick. Using a sharp knife, score the dough into 2- × 3-inch (5- × 7.5-cm) rectangles.

Dehydrate at 118°F (48°C) for several hours. Peel away from the tray liner and flip onto an unlined tray. Let dry for another 4 to 5 hours until thoroughly dry. Break at the score lines into rectangular crackers.

Store any leftovers at room temperature in a lidded container.

YIELD: ABOUT 48 CRACKERS

Italian Chia Nut Crackers

These little crackers are heavier and more substantial and can stand up to heavy dips or toppings. They're quite flavorful and are excellent with a dollop of tapenade (see page 133) or just chopped tomatoes.

- **1 cup (145 g) almonds or cashews, soaked overnight and drained**
- **1 cup (100 g) ground chia seeds**
- **½ cup (165 g) whole chia seeds**
- **½ cup (70 g) sesame seeds**
- **1 cup (100 g) chopped scallions**
- **1 teaspoon minced fresh garlic**
- **1 tablespoon (7 g) onion powder**
- **1 teaspoon garlic powder**
- **1 tablespoon (2 g) dried basil**
- **1 teaspoon salt**
- **½ teaspoon black pepper**

In a bowl, combine all ingredients, and mix until a thick dough forms. Spread the dough out on a lined dehydrator tray about ⅛-inch (3-mm) thick. Using a sharp knife, score the dough into 2- × 3-inch (5- × 7.5-cm) rectangles or triangles.

Dehydrate at 118°F (48°C) for several hours. Peel away from the tray liner and flip onto an unlined tray. Let dry for another 4 to 5 hours until thoroughly dry.

Break at the score lines into rectangular or tirangular crackers.

Store any leftovers at room temperature in a lidded container.

YIELD: ABOUT 36 TO 48 CRACKERS

Sweet Flax and Walnut Crackers

A sweet cracker is a nice change from the usual savory ones. This sweet one goes well with most cheese and also pairs nicely with the Apple Chutney. (See the recipe on page 133.) For an interesting variation, add 2 teaspoons cinnamon to the recipe.

1   **cup (100 g) finely ground flaxseeds**

½   **cup (84 g) whole flaxseeds**

1   **cup (100 g) walnuts, soaked and dried and then finely ground**

½   **cup (120 ml) agave**

¼   **cup (65 g) date paste (See how-to on page 130.)**

1   **cup (235 ml) water**

1   **teaspoon salt**

In a bowl, combine all ingredients, and mix until a thick dough forms. Spread the dough out on a lined dehydrator tray about ⅛-inch (3-mm) thick. Using a sharp knife, score the dough into 2- × 3-inch (5 × 7.5 cm) rectangles or triangles.

Dehydrate at 118°F (48°C) for several hours. Peel away from the tray liner and flip onto an unlined tray. Let dry for another 4 to 5 hours until thoroughly dry. Break at the score lines into rectangular or tirangular crackers.

Store any leftovers at room temperature in a lidded container.

YIELD: ABOUT 30 TO 32 CRACKERS

Cheesy Buckwheat Crackers

Nutritional yeast gives these light and tasty crackers a deliciously cheesy taste.

- **1 cup (100 g) buckwheat, soaked and dried**
- **1 cup (100 g) ground flaxseeds**
- **¼ cup (40 g) nutritional yeast**
- **2 tablespoons (30 ml) soy sauce or tamari**
- **1 teaspoon minced fresh garlic**
- **1½ cups (355 ml) water, or more for mixing**
- **1 teaspoon salt**

In a bowl, combine all ingredients, and mix until a sticky dough forms. Spread the dough out on a lined dehydrator tray about ⅛-inch (3 mm) thick. Using a sharp knife, score the dough into 1- to 2-inch (2.5 to 5 cm) squares.

Dehydrate at 118°F (48°C) for several hours. Peel the cracker away from the tray liner and flip onto an unlined tray. Let dry for another 4 to 5 hours until thoroughly dry. Break at the score lines into square crackers.

Store any leftovers at room temperature in a lidded container.

YIELD: ABOUT 24 CRACKERS

Basic Kale Chips

Kale chips are the ultimate raw food treat. They're crunchy, flavorful, and can be adapted a hundred different ways. Make them spicy or sweet or any other way you like them. Not only are they almost endlessly versatile, but they have a healthy dose of vitamin K, antioxidants, and fiber. Try to beat that, packaged chips!

1 **pound (455 g) fresh chopped kale**

3 **tablespoons (45 ml) olive oil**

3 **tablespoons (45 ml) agave**

3 **tablespoons (45 ml) balsamic vinegar**

1 **teaspoon salt**

Wash the kale well and pat dry. Remove the stems and also remove any of the thicker veins. Leave the leaves as large and whole as possible. Place the leaves in a large bowl.

In a small bowl, whisk together the oil, agave, vinegar, and salt. Then pour over the kale.

Use your hands to gently massage the dressing into the kale leaves. Make sure all the leaves are evenly coated. Place the coated leaves on a lined dehydrator tray, and dry at 118°F (48°C) until the kale is crispy, which will take about 8 hours or overnight.

Place any leftovers in a lidded container and store at room temperature for up to a few days.

YIELD: ABOUT 8 OUNCES (225 G)

Wash fresh kale and pat dry.

Remove the stems and larger veins.

Coat the leaves with your choice of flavorings or dressing.

Spread out on lined dehydrator trays and dry at 118°F (48°C) for 8 hours or overnight.

Nacho Cheese Kale Chips

If I were stranded on a deserted island and could only have one prepared raw treat, this would be it. This is my absolute favorite kale chip recipe, and I think you'll like it, too. It's so much like a commercial nacho-flavored cheese chip that it's easy to forget that it's also ridiculously healthy.

- **1   pound (455 g) fresh chopped kale**
- **½   cup (40 g) sundried tomatoes, soaked in water for 1 hour and drained**
- **½   cup (75 g) chopped red bell pepper**
- **½   cup (35 g) nutritional yeast**
- **¼   cup (60 ml) olive oil**
- **¼   cup (45 g) dates, chopped**
- **1   tablespoon (15 ml) soy sauce or tamari**
- **1   tablespoon (15 ml) balsamic vinegar**
- **1   teaspoon salt**
- **½   cup (120 ml) water more or less for blending**

Wash the kale and remove the stems and large veins.

In a high-powered blender, process the remaining ingredients until very smooth, adding more water if necessary for blending. Pour over the kale leaves and massage until all the leaves are well coated.

Spread the leaves out on a lined dehydrator sheet, and dry at 118°F (48°C) for about 6 hours, or until the kale is crispy.

Store leftover kale chips in a lidded container at room temperature for up to a few days.

YIELD: ABOUT 8 OUNCES (225 G)

Cool Ranch Kale Chips

Creamy ranch and kale go together wonderfully well.

- **1 pound (455 g) fresh chopped kale**
- **½ cup (75 g) cashews, soaked for 30 minutes and drained**
- **½ cup (120 ml) water**
- **2 tablespoons (30 ml) lemon juice**
- **1 tablespoon (7 g) onion powder**
- **1 tablespoon (9 g) garlic powder**
- **1 teaspoon dried dill**
- **½ teaspoon dried basil**
- **½ teaspoon dried oregano**
- **1 teaspoon salt**
- **½ teaspoon black pepper**

Wash the kale and remove the stems and veins. Pat the kale dry and place in a large bowl.

In a high-powered blender, blend the remaining ingredients until very smooth and pour over the kale, massaging to coat the leaves evenly.

Place the kale on a lined dehydrator sheet and dry at 118°F (48°C) for about 6 hours, or until the kale is crispy.

Store leftover kale chips in a lidded container at room temperature for up to a few days.

YIELD: ABOUT 8 OUNCES (225 G)

Lemony Kale Chips

These lemony kale chips are super light, refreshing and easy to make.

- **1 pound (455 g) fresh chopped kale**
- **¼ cup (60 ml) lemon juice**
- **1 teaspoon lemon zest**
- **¼ cup (60 ml) agave**
- **1 teaspoon garlic powder**
- **1 teaspoon salt**

Wash the kale and remove the stems and larger veins. Pat the kale dry and place in a large bowl.

In a smaller bowl, whisk together the remaining ingredients, and pour over the kale. Massage until the leaves are well coated.

Spread the leaves out on lined dehydrator sheets. Dry the kale at 118°F (48°C) for about 6 hours, or until the kale is crispy.

Store leftover kale chips in a lidded container at room temperature for up to a few days.

YIELD: ABOUT 8 OUNCES (225 G)

Sweet Mustard Kale Chips

These are delicately sweet and just mustardy enough.

- 1 **pound (455 g) fresh chopped kale**
- ¼ **cup (60 ml) agave**
- 1 **tablespoon (9 g) dried mustard**
- 1 **tablespoon (15 ml) balsamic vinegar**
- 1 **teaspoon onion powder**
- 1 **teaspoon salt**

Wash the kale and remove the stems and veins. Pat the kale dry and place in a large bowl.

In another bowl, whisk together the remaining ingredients, and pour over the kale, massaging to coat the leaves evenly.

Place the kale on a lined dehydrator sheet and dry at 118°F (48°C) for about 6 hours, or until the kale is crispy.

Store leftover kale chips in a lidded container at room temperature for up to a few days.

YIELD: ABOUT 8 OUNCES (225 G)

Jalapeño and Lime Kale Chips

Sweet and spicy, these kale chips are delicious and won't last long.

- 1 **pound (455 g) fresh chopped kale**
- ¼ **cup (60 ml) lime juice**
- 1 **teaspoon lime zest**
- 3 **tablespoons (45 ml) agave**
- 3 **tablespoons (45 ml) olive oil**
- 1 **teaspoon finely chopped jalapeño pepper**
- ½ **teaspoon chipotle seasoning**
- 1 **teaspoon salt**

Wash the kale and remove the stems and veins. Pat the kale dry and place in a large bowl.

In another bowl, whisk together the remaining ingredients, and pour over the kale, massaging to coat the leaves evenly.

Place the kale on a lined dehydrator sheet, and dry at 118°F (48°C) for about 6 hours, or until the kale is crispy.

Store leftover kale chips in a lidded container at room temperature for up to a few days.

YIELD: ABOUT 8 OUNCES (225 G)

chapter

11

Condiments, Sweeteners, Salsas & Chutneys

Condiments, sweeteners, salsas, and chutneys help enhance the flavor of foods. Making your own raw condiments is a healthy alternative to commercial concoctions that often contain ingredients such as high-fructose corn syrup, monosodium glutamate, and other chemicals that are best avoided. The good news is it's easy to make any raw food condiment.

Make your own healthy sweeteners using simple and pure ingredients such as dates. Date paste is a delicious, sweet addition to a raw food pantry and is super simple to make. Vanilla powder is also a delightful addition to smoothies and desserts.

Salsas add interest, texture, and vibrant flavor to any main dish, and also pair fantastically with any chip or cracker. Chutneys pack a lot of taste and can enhance any dish.

Ketchup

This super-easy raw ketchup is delicious and goes well on any raw burger or wrap.

- ½ cup (50 g) sun-dried tomatoes, chopped
- 1 cup (180 g) peeled, seeded, and chopped Roma tomatoes
- 6 dates, softened in water for 30 minutes
- 2 tablespoons (30 ml) apple cider vinegar
- 1 teaspoon fresh minced garlic
- 1 teaspoon salt

In a blender, puree all ingredients until very smooth and the consistency of ketchup. Store the ketchup in a covered container in the refrigerator for up to 1 week.

YIELD: ABOUT 1½ CUPS (360 G)

Mustard

Turmeric gives this mustard a familiar bright yellow color. It can be used on burgers and in vinaigrettes.

- ½ cup (88 g) brown mustard seeds
- ¼ cup (44 g) yellow mustard seeds
- 1½ cups (355 ml) apple cider vinegar or white wine vinegar
- 1 tablespoon (15 ml) agave
- ½ teaspoon ground turmeric
- 1 teaspoon salt
- 1 cup (235 ml) water

In a medium bowl, combine all ingredients, and allow them to stand at room temperature for 24 hours. Then pour the mixture into a small blender and puree for several minutes until mostly smooth. (The mustard will remain a little grainy.)

Store the mustard in the refrigerator in a covered container for up to 6 weeks.

YIELD: ABOUT 1 CUP (180 G)

Tip

For a tasty, sweet "honey" mustard, mix together equal parts finished mustard and agave or other liquid sweetener.

Mayonnaise

This is a creamy and mild mayo and is perfect for sandwiches, dressings, and dips.

- 1   **cup (135 g) macadamia nuts or cashews**
- 1   **cup (235 ml) water**
- 1   **teaspoon fresh minced garlic**
- 1   **tablespoon (15 ml) apple cider vinegar**
- 1   **teaspoon agave**
- ½   **teaspoon salt**

In a blender, puree all ingredients until very smooth and creamy.

Store the mayo in a covered container in the refrigerator for up to 1 week.

YIELD: ABOUT 2 CUPS (450 G)

Tip
Make a sweeter type of mayo by adding 2 tablespoons (30 ml) agave before blending.

Sweet Pickle Relish

Pickling cucumbers will work best for this recipe, but any cucumber can be used. This is great for salads and can be added to the Thousand Island recipe on page 75 for extra deliciousness.

- 2   **cups (240 g) finely chopped cucumbers**
- ¼   **cup (60 ml) agave**
- 3   **tablespoons (45 ml) apple cider vinegar**
- 1   **teaspoon salt**

Mix all ingredients until well combined. Allow to marinate for a day or so before using.

Store the relish in a lidded container in the refrigerator for up to a week.

YIELD: ABOUT 2 CUPS (490 G)

Barbecue Sauce

This barbecue sauce is rich, savory, and sweet. It goes great on any walnut or lentil loaf. Use it as a marinade for any vegetables, and then dehydrate them for an hour or so to warm them. Delish!

- ½   **cup (40 g) sun-dried tomatoes, soaked to soften if necessary**
- 1   **cup (180 g) peeled, seeded, and chopped Roma tomatoes**
- 6   **dates, soaked in water for 30 minutes and drained**
- ¼   **cup (60 ml) apple cider vinegar**
- 2   **teaspoons fresh minced garlic**
- 3   **tablespoons (30 g) minced onion**
- 1   **teaspoon salt**
- ¼   **cup (60 ml) olive oil**
- ½   **cup (120 ml) water, for blending**

In a blender, puree all ingredients until very smooth. Add more or less water as necessary for blending.

Store the barbecue sauce in a covered container in the refrigerator for up to a week.

YIELD: ABOUT 1¾ CUPS (530 G)

Date Paste

Date paste is an excellent thick liquid sweetener and can often be used in place of agave.

- **2 cups (360 g) dates**
- **1 cup (235) water, more or less, for blending**

In a blender, puree the dates and water until very smooth. Add more water if necessary to facilitate blending.

Store the date paste in a covered container in the refrigerator for up to 1 week.

YIELD: ABOUT 2½ CUPS (650 G)

Caramel Dip

This sweet treat goes really well with apple slices or as a dip for any fruit.

- **1 cup (180 g) dates, soaked in water for 30 minutes and drained**
- **2 tablespoons (32 g) almond butter**
- **½ cup (120 ml) almond milk or flax milk, plus more for blending**
- **Pinch of salt**

In a blender, purée all ingredients until very smooth. Add more almond milk or flax milk as needed for blending.

Store any leftover caramel dip in a covered container in the refrigerator for up to 1 week.

YIELD: ABOUT 1 CUP (225 G)

Balsamic Date Syrup

This sweet and vinegary syrup can be used to make dressings, or used as is. It's wonderful drizzled over a bowl of fruit.

- 1 cup (180 g) dates, soaked in water for 30 minutes and drained
- 1 cup (235 ml) balsamic vinegar

In a blender, puree the dates and vinegar until smooth.

Store the balsamic date syrup in a covered container in the refrigerator for up to 2 weeks.

YIELD: ABOUT 1¾ CUPS (400 G)

Coconut Butter

There is no recipe needed to make coconut butter. There is only one ingredient, and that's coconut. Maybe two ingredients are necessary, because you will also need time. Oh, you'll also need patience.

- 4 cups (340 g) unsweetened dried coconut flakes

In a food processor fitted with an "S" blade, process the dried coconut flakes until they turn into coconut butter. (This will take at least several minutes and as long as 20 minutes, and it will seem as though it will never turn to coconut butter. This is where the patience is needed. It will turn from flaky to grainy and finally to creamy and will transform into a beautiful batch of coconut butter.) Scrape down the sides as needed while processing. The mixture will heat up as it processes, so stop the machine and allow the coconut to cool down if needed.

Store coconut butter in a lidded glass jar at room temperature for up to a month and in the refrigerator or freezer for 3 months.

YIELD: ABOUT 2½ CUPS (650 G)

Vanilla Powder

Add this delicious powder to smoothies and desserts or use in place of vanilla extract.

- 1 cup (100 g) buckwheat groats, soaked and dehydrated until very dry
- 6 whole vanilla beans, cut into 1-inch (2.5 cm) sections

This works best in a spice or coffee grinder, but a high-powered blender can also be used. Process the buckwheat groats and the vanilla beans until powdered. (It may have to be done in batches if using a small spice grinder.)

Store the vanilla powder at room temperature in an airtight container for up to a few weeks.

YIELD: ABOUT 1 CUP (120 G)

Crème Anglaise

Crème Anglaise is a wonderful accompaniment to pies and other desserts and works especially well with chocolate.

- 1 cup (130 g) macadamia nuts or cashews
- ½ cup (325 g) coconut butter
- ¼ cup (60 ml) agave
- 1 teaspoon vanilla extract or vanilla powder
- 1 cup (235 ml) water
  Pinch of salt

In a blender, puree all ingredients until very smooth.

Store the Crème Anglaise in a covered container in the refrigerator for up to 1 week.

YIELD: ABOUT 1½ CUPS (390 G)

Fruit and Berry Jam

Nearly any fruit or berry can be blended with dates to make a fantastic and naturally sweet and gooey jam.

1   cup (180 g) dates, soaked in water for 30 minutes and drained well
1   cup (145 g) any fruit or berries
2   tablespoons (30 ml) lemon juice
    Pinch of salt
    Water, for blending

In a blender, puree all ingredients until very smooth. Add water for blending, only using as much as necessary.

Store the jam in a covered container in the refrigerator for up to 2 weeks.

YIELD: ABOUT 1¾ CUPS (560 G)

Mango Peach Salsa

Deliciously sweet and spicy, this fruity salsa can be served with crackers or breads and also goes well on cucumber slices.

1   cup (175 g) chopped mango
2   ripe medium peaches, chopped
¼   cup (40 g) chopped red onion
3   tablespoons (45 ml) lime juice
1   teaspoon lime zest
1   tablespoon (15 ml) agave
2   tablespoons (6 g) chopped fresh basil
½   teaspoon salt
½   teaspoon black pepper
½   teaspoon crushed red-pepper flakes

In a bowl, combine all ingredients and gently stir to mix. Allow to stand for 1 to 2 hours before serving.

Store any leftover salsa in a covered container in the refrigerator for up to 1 week.

YIELD: ABOUT 2 CUPS (200 G)

Tomato Watermelon Salsa

This light and refreshing salsa goes well on any raw cracker and also makes a fine topping for tomato or cucumber slices.

2   medium tomatoes, chopped
1   cup (150 g) chopped watermelon
3   tablespoons (30 g) chopped red onion
1   jalapeño pepper, minced
3   tablespoons (45 ml) lime juice
1   teaspoon lime zest
1   tablespoon (1 g) chopped fresh cilantro
½   teaspoon salt
½   teaspoon black pepper
½   teaspoon crushed red-pepper flakes

In a bowl, combine all ingredients and gently stir to mix. Allow to stand 1 to 2 hours before serving.

Store any leftover salsa in a covered container in the refrigerator for up to 1 week.

YIELD: ABOUT 2½ CUPS (220 G)

Tip

For smooth, seedless jams, puree and strain fruit or berries, and then blend with the softened dates.

Green and Black Olive Tapenade

The name of this dish comes from the Provençal word for capers, which is *tapenas*. Traditionally, it also contains anchovies, but this is a healthy, fish-free version and can be used on crackers and breads.

- 1   cup (100 g) chopped green olives
- 1   cup (100 g) black olives
- 1   teaspoon fresh minced garlic
- ¼   cup (20 g) sun-dried tomatoes
- 2   tablespoons (16 g) capers
- ¼   cup (60 ml) olive oil
- 1   tablespoon (3 g) fresh basil
-     Salt, to taste

In a food processor fitted with an "S" blade, gently pulse all ingredients until the pieces are small but the mixture is still chunky. Olives are generally very salty, but if yours are not, add a little salt to your tapenade as needed.

Store any leftover tapenade in a covered container in the refrigerator for up to 1 week.

YIELD: ABOUT 2¼ CUPS (220 G)

Apple Chutney

Chutneys are sweet and spicy blends that originated in East Indian cuisine. A perfect way to use them is a dollop on the side of your favorite dish.

- 4   medium apples, peeled, cored, and chopped
- ¼   cup (60 ml) agave
- ¼   cup (40 g) chopped red onion
- 5   dates, chopped
- 1   teaspoon orange zest
- 1   teaspoon grated fresh ginger
- ½   teaspoon ground cinnamon
- ¼   cup (25 g) pecans

In a food processor fitted with an "S" blade, gently pulse all ingredients except the pecans until well chopped and the apples and dates are in small pieces. Add the pecans and pulse another few times.

Store any leftover chutney in a covered container in the refrigerator for up to 1 week.

YIELD: MAKES ABOUT 2 CUPS (200 G)

12

chapter

> " Many's the long night I've dreamed of cheese … "
>
> —Robert Louis Stevenson, novelist, poet, and author of *Treasure Island*

Cheeses

Cheese and dairy can be the most difficult food to give up when committing to a vegan and plant-based diet. There's a good reason for that. The digestion of casein, the protein in dairy, creates casomorpins, which have an opiate and addictive effect on our bodies.

There are many good reasons to abstain from cow's milk. Dairy consumption is closely linked with osteoporosis. Animal-based protein inhibits the formation of bone and accelerates its breakdown, which leads to decreased bone density. Conventional dairy is also implicated in high cholesterol, heart disease, breast cancer, prostate cancer, obesity, and intestinal and autoimmune disorders.

Dairy can be easily and deliciously replaced with vegan nut cheese, yogurts, milks, and creams. Nuts are rich in energy, protein, antioxidants, minerals, and the super-healthy omega-3 fatty acids. They contain B vitamins, vitamin E, manganese, potassium, calcium, iron, magnesium, zinc, fluoride, and selenium, as well as oleic and palmitoleic acids, which lower LDL or "bad" cholesterol and raise HDL or "good" cholesterol. Nuts can help prevent heart disease and strokes and promote a healthy blood lipid profile.

Most of the cheese recipes here call for probiotic powder. As the bacteria in the probiotic grow, they produce the tangy flavor that will give vegan cheese its bite. You can buy probiotics in loose powdered form or in capsules. The loose powder is the most economical and the easiest to use; the capsules will need to be opened. If you have no probiotic powder, though, don't despair. The cheeses taste great without it. Just follow the recipe as is, but leave out the probiotic powder. See the resources section on page 172 for information on where to buy it.

Basic Nut Cheese

This simple nut cheese can be made with cashews or almonds and is fabulous on crackers and in salads. Most raw cheese recipes will follow this basic technique. The variations are almost endless. Add your favorite herbs and spices, chopped sun-dried tomatoes, or even fruit and dates for a sweet cheese. Chives, tarragon, and basil are good choices. You can also roll the cheese in cracked black pepper or crushed red-pepper flakes.

- 2 cups (290 g) cashews or almonds, soaked overnight and drained
- ½ cup (120 ml) water, or more for blending
- 1 tablespoon (15 ml) lemon juice
- 1 teaspoon probiotic powder
- 1 tablespoon (10 g) nutritional yeast
- 1 teaspoon salt
- 3 tablespoons (3 g) chopped fresh herbs or 2 tablespoons (4 g) dried herbs (optional)

Place the cashews, water, and lemon juice in a food processor or blender. Process until very creamy, adding more water if necessary. Add the probiotic powder and pulse a few times to mix well.

Pour the mix into a lidded glass container and allow to sit at room temperature for 12 to 24 hours.

Once the cheese has sat out and developed a tangy taste, spoon it into several layers of cheesecloth. Wrap the cheesecloth securely around the cheese and twist into a tight ball, then flatten it to make a round. Place the wrapped cheese in a colander or large strainer.

Place a couple of heavy plates or a water-filled bowl on top of the cheese. (This will press it and cause the extra moisture to drain away.) Allow the cheese to drain for about 4 hours.

Once drained, mix in the nutritional yeast and salt, and stir until well incorporated. Then shape the cheese into a round wheel or a log shape.

Roll the cheese in the herbs, if using.

YIELD: ABOUT 2¼ CUPS (300 G)

Tip

An optional step for a very white cheese is to blanch the almonds first, though it might not be considered a raw technique. Blanching heats the skins of the almonds and allows them to be easily peeled. The high temperature is concentrated in the very outer layer of the almond and doesn't heat the inside to any great degree. To blanch, place the almonds in a glass or metal bowl. Pour boiling water over the almonds and let them stand for 2 minutes. Quickly drain the water and pour cold water over the almonds to cool them. The skins should slip off very easily now.

Creamy Cheddar Spread

Super-fast, this easy cheese spread can be made and ready to serve in just minutes. Use it on crackers, in wraps, or as a cheesy vegetable dip.

- **2 cups (290 g) cashews or almonds, soaked overnight**
- **½ cup (120 ml) carrot juice**
- **¼ cup (60 ml) lemon juice**
- **¼ cup (30g) nutritional yeast**
- **1 teaspoon salt**

In a food processor fitted with an "S" blade, or a high-powered blender, process all ingredients until very smooth and creamy.

Store leftovers in a lidded container for up to 1 week.

YIELD: MAKES ABOUT 2¼ CUPS (300 G)

Nutrition FYI: Nutritional Yeast

Nutritional yeast is an inactive yeast usually grown on beet sugar. It contains B vitamins, folic acid, minerals, protein, and fiber, and is deliciously cheesy!

Very Sharp Cheddar

Carrot juice gives this Cheddar the characteristic orange color, and finishing it off in the dehydrator will make it firmer and slightly crusty on the outside.

2 cups (290 g) cashews, soaked overnight and drained
½ cup (120 ml) carrot juice, more for blending
1 tablespoon (15 ml) lemon juice
1 teaspoon probiotic powder
¼ cup (40 g) nutritional yeast
1 teaspoon salt

In a food processor fitted with an "S" blade, process the cashews, carrot juice, and lemon juice until the mix is very smooth. (This may take several minutes, depending on your machine.) Add water for blending, if necessary.

When smooth, add the probiotic powder and pulse a few times to blend. Pour into a lidded glass container and cover. Allow to sit at room temperature for 24 hours.

Spoon the cheese mix into cheesecloth and wrap tightly. Place it in a colander and put something heavy on top of it. This could be a few plates or a water-filled jug or bowl. Allow to drain for several hours.

Add the nutritional yeast and salt, and stir well to combine thoroughly. Then shape the cheese into a wheel shape. Place the cheese wheel into the dehydrator, and dry at 118°F (48°C) for about 4 hours.

Store tightly wrapped in the refrigerator for up to 1 week.

YIELD: ABOUT 2¼ CUPS (270 G)

Hot and Spicy Cheese

Hot enough for ya'? Cayenne and jalapeño peppers make this cheese super-spicy. Adjust the heat to your liking by adding more or less cayenne powder.

1 cup (135 g) macadamia nuts, soaked overnight and drained
1 cup (145 g) cashews, soaked overnight and drained
½ cup (120 ml) carrot juice
1 teaspoon probiotic powder
2 tablespoons (30 ml) lemon juice
2 tablespoons agave (28 ml)
1 teaspoon salt
½ to 1 teaspoon cayenne pepper or more, to taste
1 tablespoon (9 g) finely minced jalapeño pepper

In a food processor fitted with an "S" blade, process the macadamias, cashews, and carrot juice until very smooth and creamy. Add the probiotic powder and pulse several times to incorporate.

Pour into a lidded, glass container and let sit at room temperature for 24 hours.

Spoon the cheese mixture into several layers of cheesecloth and wrap tightly. Place in a colander with a heavy weight on top. Allow to drain for 12 to 24 hours.

Remove the cheese from the cheesecloth, and add the agave, salt, cayenne, and jalapeño. Mix well to combine. Form into a wheel or log shape. Leftover cheese can be stored in a lidded container in the refrigerator for up to 1 week.

YIELD: ABOUT 2½ CUPS (300 G)

Nutritional FYI: Carrot Juice

The carrot juice in this recipe adds another layer of nutrition. Carrots contain the phytonutrients beta-carotene and lutein and can help prevent vision loss. They've also been shown to prevent several cancers as well as infections. Carrots can reduce the risk of lung cancer by as much as 50 percent.

Sun-Dried Tomato Cheese

Sun-dried tomatoes and chipotle give this cheese a nice, smoky flavor. Almonds make a stiffer, less-creamy cheese. For a creamier cheese, use cashews.

- 2 **cups (290 g) almonds or cashews, soaked overnight and drained**
- ½ **cup (120 ml) water, or more for blending**
- 3 **tablespoons (45 ml) lemon juice**
- 1 **teaspoon probiotic powder**
- 1 **teaspoon minced fresh garlic**
- ½ **teaspoon chipotle powder**
- 1 **teaspoon salt**
- ½ **cup (30 g) sun-dried tomatoes (See how to on page 44), soaked for 30 minutes, dried well, and chopped**

In a food processor fitted with an "S" blade or a high-powered blender, process the almonds, water, and lemon juice until very smooth. Add more water if necessary for blending. Add the probiotic powder and pulse a few times to blend well.

Pour the cheese mix into a lidded glass container and allow to sit at room temperature for 24 hours to develop a tangy taste.

Spoon the cheese into several layers of cheesecloth. Wrap the cheesecloth tightly around the cheese, and place it in a colander. Place something heavy on top of the wrapped cheese, such as plates or a water-filled jug. Let drain for several hours or overnight.

Once the cheese has drained and is fairly firm, add the garlic, chipotle powder, and salt and mix well. (The sun-dried tomatoes will be soaking.) Drain them and pat them dry. Then chop the tomatoes and mix into the cheese until well incorporated.

The cheese can be served like this, or it can be placed in the dehydrator for 4 hours at 118°F (48°C) until a hardened skin has formed.

Store leftovers in a lidded container in the refrigerator for up to 1 week.

YIELD: ABOUT 2¼ CUPS (270 G)

Nutrition FYI: Tomatoes

Tomatoes are an outstanding source of lycopene and other antioxidants and have been linked to heart health. Tomatoes can help lower cholesterol and triglycerides, prevent stroke, and even improve bone health.

Creamy "Salty" Cheese

This creamy cheese is a lot like goat's milk cheese. It's delicious made into a wheel or log, or it can be broken into small pieces and dehydrated for firmer cheese crumbles.

- **2 cups (290 g) cashews, soaked overnight and drained**
- **½ cup (120 ml) water**
- **2 tablespoons (30 ml) lemon juice**
- **1 teaspoon probiotic powder**
- **1 tablespoon (10 g) nutritional yeast**
- **1½ teaspoons salt**

In a food processor fitted with an "S" blade, process the cashews, water, and lemon juice until very smooth. Add in the probiotic powder, and pulse a few times to mix well. Pour into a lidded glass container and let sit at room temperature for 24 hours.

Spoon the cheese mixture into several layers of cheesecloth and wrap tightly. Place in a colander or strainer and place a heavy weight on top of the cheese. Allow to drain for about 8 hours.

Once drained, add in the nutritional yeast and salt, and mix until well incorporated. Roll into a log shape.

This cheese can be used as is, or can be dehydrated for several hours until a crust forms. Or, the cheese can be broken into small pieces and dehydrated for several hours to make slightly crunchy cheese crumbles.

YIELD: 2 CUPS (120 G)

Garlic and Chives Cream Cheese Spread

This garlicky spread goes great on any cracker or wrap and can be slightly thinned with water, almond milk, or flax milk to make a fabulous vegetable dip.

- 2 cups (290 g) cashews or almonds
- 1 cup (235 ml) water
- 1 teaspoon probiotic powder
- 1 teaspoon salt
- 3 tablespoons (45 ml) lemon juice
- 3 tablespoons (30 g) nutritional yeast
- 2 teaspoons minced fresh garlic
- 3 tablespoons (9 g) chopped fresh chives

In a food processor fitted with an "S" blade, process the cashews, water, and probiotic powder until very smooth. This may take several minutes depending on your machine.

Pour into a lidded container and allow to sit at room temperature for 24 hours.

Add the remaining ingredients and stir to mix well.

Store leftover spread in a lidded container in the refrigerator for up to 1 week.

YIELD: 3 CUPS (360 G)

Nutrition FYI: Chives and Garlic

Chives and garlic are members of the allium family. They contain antioxidants known as thiosulfinites, which convert to allicin. Allicin has been shown to reduce cholesterol and is anti viral, anti bacterial, and anti-fungal. It also reduces blood pressure and increases elasticity in blood vessels.

Nutrition FYI: Blueberries
Blueberries are full of powerful antioxidants and can help improve vision and prevent macular degeneration as well as improve motor skills and reverse age-related short-term memory loss.

Quick Coconut Macadamia Yogurt with Strawberries

This yogurt is fast, and there's no need to wait for probiotics to culture. Lemon juice provides the tang here.

- 1 **cup (135 g) macadamia nuts, soaked for several hours, and drained**
- 1 **cup (235 ml) water**
- 2 **tablespoons (30 ml) lemon juice**
- 2 **tablespoons (30 ml) coconut oil**
- ½ **teaspoon salt**
- 1 **cup (170 g) chopped strawberries**
- 1 **tablespoon (15 ml) agave**
- 3 **tablespoons (45 ml) agave**

In a food processor fitted with an "S" blade or a high-powered blender, process the macadamia nuts, water, lemon juice, coconut oil, and salt until very creamy. Divide into four bowls.

In a bowl, mash the strawberries and the agave with a fork until a chunky jam-like consistency forms. Pour a few spoonfuls over each bowl of yogurt.

YIELD: ABOUT FOUR ½-CUP (240 G) SERVINGS

Tip
Macadamia nuts are often quite expensive. For more economy, cashews can be substituted for the macadamias.

Blueberry Fool

A "fool" is a Greek yogurt dish that is layered parfait-style. Greek yogurt is traditionally very thick. Make your "fool" thinner if you wish by adding more water.

- 1 **cup (145 g) cashews, soaked overnight and drained**
- ¾ **cup (175 ml) water**
- 3 **tablespoons (45 ml) agave**
- 2 **tablespoons (30 ml) lemon juice**
- ½ **teaspoon salt**
- 1 **cup (145 g) blueberries, fresh, or frozen and thawed, divided**
- 1 **tablespoon (7 g) chopped walnuts**

In a food processor fitted with an "S" blade or a high-powered blender, process the cashews, water, agave, lemon juice, and salt until very smooth and creamy.

Divide the yogurt mixture in half, and set half aside. To the remaining half of the mix, add ½ cup (75 g) of the blueberries and process again until very smooth. (This will be a blueberry yogurt.)

Layer the white yogurt and the blueberry yogurt into 2 to 4 small bowls or parfait glasses. Top with a few of the remaining blueberries and the walnuts.

YIELD: ABOUT 2 CUPS (240 G)

13

Desserts

> "Life is uncertain. Eat dessert first."
>
> —Ernestine Ulmer, American author

Pies and tarts and brownies—oh my! Raw food desserts can be as simple as fresh fruit or as decadent as a creamy cheesecake. Because they are free of refined sugar and heavily processed ingredients, and don't rely on butter, eggs, or flour, enjoying raw desserts can be a guilt-free and healthy indulgence.

It's in our nature to have a sweet tooth; we're born with it. Human breast milk is sweet and helps ensure that babies seek that nourishment and thrive. We also have a long history with sweet things. Ancient civilizations used nuts and fruits as desserts, and they were considered the first candies. The first apple pie recipe was printed in 1381. The word *dessert* came about in the sixteenth century from the Old French word, *desservir*, and the first ice creams date back to the fourth century BCE.

Nuts and dates in a food processor will make the quick and almost effortless pie crusts commonly used in raw desserts. Pie crusts can be made of equal parts of any nuts paired with a sticky, dried fruit such as dates or raisins. Nuts can be used to make a delightful cheesecake filling as well.

Fruit is also quite versatile in raw desserts, and it can be used in tarts, pies, and crumbles, as well as on its own. Luscious raw ice cream can be made with as little as one magical ingredient. (Spoiler alert—it's bananas!)

Raw food desserts are amazing. They're great tasting and good for you. Enjoy!

Easy Banana Ice Cream

Something magical happens to bananas when they're frozen. They become sweet, creamy little nuggets that make perfectly textured raw ice cream.

To make icecream using a food processor fitted with an "S" blade, first process the bananas into ice cream. Then add in your preferred flavoring ingredients and continue processing until smooth and well incorporated. The taste combinations are nearly endless, but here are a few suggestions to get you started.

Vanilla

- 4 **large bananas, sliced and frozen**
- 2 **teaspoons vanilla powder (See recipe on page 131.)**

Maple Pecan

- 4 **large bananas, sliced and frozen**
- 3 **tablespoons (45 ml) maple syrup**
- ½ **cup (55 g) chopped pecans**

Chocolate

- 4 **large bananas, sliced and frozen**
- 3 **tablespoons (45 ml) agave**
- ¼ **teaspoon vanilla powder or 1 teaspoon vanilla extract**
- ¼ **cup (20 g) cacao powder**

Cherry Vanilla

- 4 **large bananas, sliced and frozen**
- 1 **cup (155 g) frozen cherries**
- ¼ **teaspoon vanilla powder or 1 teaspoon vanilla extract**

Strawberry Lemon

- 4 **large bananas, sliced and frozen**
- 3 **tablespoons (45 ml) lemon juice**
- 1 **cup (255 g) frozen strawberries**

YIELD: EACH BANANA ICE CREAM RECIPE MAKES ABOUT 4 SERVINGS.

Pistachio Ice Cream

Avocado gives this salty and sweet ice cream a green tint and also adds a delightful creaminess.

- 4 **ripe bananas, sliced and frozen**
- 1 **ripe avocado, sliced and frozen**
- ¼ **cup (60 ml) agave**
- 1 **dropper liquid stevia**
- ½ **cup (60 g) pistachio nuts**

Place the bananas, avocado, agave, and stevia in a food processor fitted with an "S" blade, and process the ingredients until thick and creamy. Add the pistachios, and pulse them once or twice to incorporate.

YIELD: ABOUT 3 CUPS (360 G)

Slice several bananas into 1-inch (2.5-cm) chunks, and freeze for several hours or overnight.

Allow frozen banana slices to thaw slightly, for about 5 minutes. Then, in a food processor fitted with an "S" blade, process the bananas until thick, smooth, and creamy.

It will take a minute or two for the bananas to become smooth and ice cream–like. Scrape down the sides of the food processor as needed.

Be patient.

Soon, the frozen bananas will have blended into a thick, creamy treat that's also good for you.

Nutrition FYI: Bananas

When it comes to keeping the doctor away, a banana a day is even better than an apple a day. Comparing the two, bananas contain five times more beta-carotene and iron, three times as much phosphorous, more potassium, and plenty of healthy, natural sugars.

Apple Pie

Made of nothing more than fruit, nuts, and spices, this apple pie is a healthy version of the traditional favorite.

For the Crust

- ½ **cup (95 g) almonds**
- ¼ **cup (25 g) pecans**
- 1 **cup (180 g) dates**
- ½ **cup (40 g) unsweetened shredded dried coconut flakes**

For the Filling

- 6 **apples, peeled, cored, and thinly sliced**
- ¼ **cup (45 g) chopped dates**
- ¼ **cup (40 g) date paste**
- ¼ **cup (60 ml) agave**
- 2 **tablespoons (32 g) almond butter**
- 2 **tablespoons (30 ml) lemon juice**
- ¾ **teaspoon ground cinnamon**
- ½ **teaspoon ground ginger**
- ½ **teaspoon ground nutmeg**
- ½ **teaspoon allspice**
  Pinch of salt
- 3 **tablespoons (30 g) chopped candied nuts (optional)**

To make the crust: Place all of the crust ingredients into a food processor fitted with an "S" blade, and process them until the mix begins to stick together. (Don't over-process. This will take about a minute in most processors. The mixture will be crumbly.) Pour this mixture into an 8-inch (17-cm) pie plate or pan and firmly press into the bottom and up the sides. Store the crust in the refrigerator to firm while making the filling.

To make the filling: Peel, core, and slice the apples and chop the dates. Put the apples and dates in a medium bowl and set aside. Whisk together the remaining ingredients and pour over the apples and dates. Gently toss until the ingredients are combined and well coated.

Pour this mixture into the crust and spread evenly. This pie can be served immediately or refrigerated for a few hours before serving. It's beautiful on its own but also pairs well with Banana Ice Cream (see recipe on page 146) or Crème Anglaise (see recipe on page 131).

Store leftovers in an airtight container in the refrigerator for up to 1 week.

YIELD: ABOUT 8 SERVINGS

A simple and easy mix of nuts, dried coconut, and dates makes a delicious pie crust that complements almost any filling.

Place all the crust ingredients in a food processor fitted with an "S" blade.

Process until the mixture becomes crumbly and begins to stick together. Be careful not to over-process.

Pour the crust mixture into a pie plate, springform pan, or tart pan.

Press the crust into the bottom and up the sides of the pan.

Pumpkin Pie

This pumpkin pie doesn't use any actual pumpkin, but it tastes so much like the fall favorite that you'll never know the difference. Added advantage? Fresh carrots are always available, so you can enjoy this healthy pie all year long.

For the Crust

- ½ **cup (95 g) almonds**
- ½ **cup (55 g) pecans**
- 1½ **cups (270 g) dates**
- **Pinch of salt**

For the Filling

- 4 **carrots, peeled and chopped**
- ½ **cup (75 g) cashews or macadamia nuts, soaked overnight and drained**
- 6 **dates, soaked in water for 30 minutes and drained**
- ¼ **cup (60 ml) maple syrup**
- ¾ **teaspoon ground cinnamon**
- ½ **teaspoon ground nutmeg**
- ¼ **teaspoon allspice**
- 3 **tablespoons (45 ml) coconut oil**
- 1 **cup (235 ml) water, more or less for blending**
- 3 **tablespoons (30 g) chopped candied nuts, for topping (optional)**

To make the crust: Place the crust ingredients into a food processor fitted with an "S" blade, and process until finely chopped and the mix begins to stick together. Don't over-process. Pour this mixture into an 8-inch (17-cm) pie plate or 6-inch (15-cm) springform pan, and press into the bottom and up the sides. Place the crust the refrigerator to firm while making the filling.

To make the filling: Place all the filling ingredients into a blender and puree until very smooth. (This may take a few minutes.) Add more water if necessary to facilitate blending.

Pour the filling into the crust and spread evenly. Top with candied nuts, if using. (See recipe on page 47.) Place the pie in the freezer to firm for at least 1 hour. Allow to stand for a few minutes before serving. This pie goes wonderfully with a dollop of Crème Anglaise. (See recipe on page 131.) Store leftover pie tightly wrapped in the freezer for up to 1 month.

YIELD: ABOUT 6 SERVINGS

Raw Raspberry Sorbet (Nut-Free)

By Casey McCluskey

There's nothing like a sweet, creamy raw ice cream recipe to please the crowds (or eat all by yourself). The recipe is one of my very favorites for many reasons:

- It's made only with the highest quality, clean ingredients.
- It's insanely delicious. Really.
- It digests beautifully even with the fruit and fat combination (because of the low-sugar fruit, high water content in the avocado, and because avocado is in fact also a fruit).
- It uses stevia as the primary sweetener other than the berries. Stevia is an ideal sweetener if you are trying to lose weight, helps to balance blood sugar levels and diabetic conditions, and doesn't feed candida overgrowth in the body.
- It's simple and easy to make. You'll be ready to eat in 5 minutes flat.
- It uses avocado, an incredible healthy fat, and raspberries with their very high antioxidant and vitamin content.
- Kids, partners, and friends love it!

For the Sorbet

- 1 **large avocado**
- 1 **lime, juiced (or more)**
- 2 **cups (500 g) frozen raspberries**
- 1 **teaspoon vanilla extract**
- 5 to 15 **drops liquid or vanilla stevia**

For Toppings (Optional)

Fresh or frozen whole raspberries, sliced bananas, freeze-dried berries or other fruits, raw chocolate chopped into pieces, or cacao nibs

To make the sorbet: Put all the sorbet ingredients in a food processor fitted with the "S" blade or into a high-speed blender. Add the berries into the processor straight from the freezer so they add to the icy effect. Process until the mixture is only just well combined because you don't want to lose the ice cream consistency and turn it into a liquid.

To make the toppings, if using: Serve with toppings of choice, and enjoy each and every bite, guilt-free!

YIELD: 3 SERVINGS

Casey McCluskey is an acclaimed health and life coach, author, motivational speaker, and co-founder of the Weight Loss Blueprint and Vimergy, which shows you how to get radiant health and energy, lose weight, and heal naturally so that you can live the life you want in a body you love. Casey has helped thousands of people across the world achieve radiant, long-lasting physical and emotional wellness via her international private coaching, guided group programs, health education, motivational speaking, and Tonic Herb line at Vimergy.com and WeightLossBlueprint.com.

Blueberry Lemon
Swirl Cheesecake

Blueberry and lemon work together here in excellent partnership, creating the perfect blend of sweet and tart. The pale and dark purple swirls go together beautifully, as well.

For the Crust

- ½ **cup (70 g) macadamia nuts**
- ½ **cup (95 g) almonds**
- ½ **cup (40 g) unsweetened shredded dried coconut flakes**
- 1 **cup (180 g) dates**
  Pinch of salt

For the Blueberry Purée

- 1 **cup (145 g) frozen blueberries**
- ¼ **cup (60 ml) agave**

For the Filling

- 2 **cups (290 g) almonds, soaked overnight and drained**
- ¼ **cup (60 ml) lemon juice**
- 2 **teaspoons lemon zest**
- ¾ **cup (175 ml) agave**
- ¼ **cup (65 g) coconut butter**
  Pinch of salt
- 1 **cup (235 ml) water, for blending**
- 2 **tablespoons (20 g) fresh blueberries, for topping**

To make the crust: Place all the crust ingredients in a food processor fitted with an "S" blade, and process the ingredients until they are crumbly and begin to stick together. (This will take about 1 minute. Don't over-process.)

Pour the mixture a plastic wrap–lined 6-inch (15 cm) spring-form pan, and press into the bottoms and up the sides. (Lining the inside of the pan with plastic wrap will ensure the looser filling won't run out of the pan seam.)

To make the blueberry purée: Place the blueberries and agave in a small blender and puree until very smooth. Set aside.

To make the filling: Place all the filling ingredients into a food processor fitted with an "S" blade, and process until the filling is very smooth and creamy. (This may take several minutes.) Scrape down the sides as needed.

Remove about half of the filling and mix with the blueberry puree. Then drop blobs of each filling into the prepared crust. Use a knife to swirl through the different colored fillings. (But don't overwork it.) Top with a few fresh, whole blueberries.

Freeze the cheesecake for at least 3 hours. Allow to thaw for a few minutes before cutting. Store leftover cheesecake tightly wrapped in the freezer for up to 1 month.

YIELD: ABOUT 8 SERVINGS

Walnut Maple Pecan Cheesecake

Maple syrup lends a distinct and mellow sweetness to this cheesecake.

For the Crust

- ¾ cup (105 g) almonds
- ¾ cup (90 g) walnuts
- 1 cup (180 g) dates

For the Filling

- 1½ cups (220 g) almonds, soaked overnight and drained
- ½ cup (55 g) pecans
- ¼ cup (60 ml) lemon juice
- ½ cup (60 g) date paste
- ½ cup (120 ml) maple syrup
- 1 cup (235 ml) water
  Pinch of cinnamon
  Pinch of salt

For the Topping

- ¼ cup (25 g) chopped pecans
- ¼ cup (30 g) chopped walnuts
- 2 tablespoons (30 ml) maple syrup

To make the crust: In a food processor fitted with an "S" blade, process all the crust ingredients until the mixture becomes crumbly and begins to stick together. Pour into a plastic wrap–lined 6-inch (15 cm) springform pan, and press into the bottom and up the sides.

To make the filling: Place all the filling ingredients in a food processor fitted with an "S" blade, and process until very smooth. (This may take several minutes.) Scrape down the sides as needed. Pour the filling into the crust and spread evenly. Place the cheesecake in the freezer for at least 3 hours to firm. Allow to thaw for several minutes before serving.

To make the topping: Stir together the chopped nuts and maple syrup. Pour on top of the cheesecake.

Store leftover cheesecake tightly wrapped in the freezer for up to 1 month.

YIELD: ABOUT 8 SERVINGS

Mixed Fruit Tart

Fresh fruit paired with a nut-free crust makes this a light and refreshing dessert.

For the Crust

- ¾ cup (65 g) unsweetened shredded dried coconut flakes
- ½ cup (50 g) buckwheat groats, soaked and dehydrated
- 1½ cups (270 g) dates
- 2 tablespoons (30 g) coconut butter
  Pinch of salt

For the Mango Cream Filling

- 1 small banana
- 1 cup (175 g) chopped mango
- ¼ cup (60 ml) agave
- ½ teaspoon vanilla extract or vanilla powder (See recipe on page 131.)

For the Fruit Filling

- 2 nectarines, sliced
- ½ cup (75 g) sliced strawberries
- ½ cup (75 g) blackberries
- 2 kiwifruit, sliced

To make the crust: Use an 8-inch (20 cm) tart pan to make one large tart. Alternatively, use four 4-inch (10 cm) tartlet pans instead. In a food processor fitted with an "S" blade, process the crust ingredients until the mix becomes crumbly and begins to stick together. Divide the mix evenly between the pans, and press the mix into the bottom and up the sides.

To make the mango cream filling: In a food processor fitted with an "S" blade, process the banana, mango, agave, and vanilla until very smooth.

Spoon into the bottom of the prepared crusts and spread evenly.

To make the fruit filling: Prepare the fruit and arrange decoratively on top of the mango banana cream layer. These tartlets are best served right away, but can be refrigerated for up to a few days.

YIELD: 1 LARGE TART OR 4 SMALLER TARTLETS

Avocado Lime Cheesecake

By Heather Pace

This delicious and creamy recipe is elegant but not overly complicated.

For the Crust

1½	cups (220 g) almonds
⅔	cup (95 g) raisins
¼	cup (20 g) shredded coconut
1 to 2	teaspoons pure vanilla or water

For the Filling

2	medium to large avocados
6	tablespoons agave
½	cup (120 ml) lime juice
1	teaspoon pure vanilla
6	drops stevia
5	tablespoons (75 ml) melted coconut oil
¼	cup (65 g) melted coconut butter
	Lime zest

To make the crust: Grind the almonds into a flour in a food processor. Add the raisins and continue grinding until broken down. Add the coconut and vanilla or water. Grind again to incorporate. Add an additional ½ to 1 teaspoon water if needed to keep the mixture together when pressed in your hand. (I often need 2 teaspoons.) Press evenly into the bottom of a 6- or 8-inch (15- or 17-cm) springform pan (depending on how thick you want the cake).

To make the filling: Blend the avocados, agave, lime juice, vanilla, and stevia until smooth and creamy. Add the oil, butter, and some lime zest. Blend to incorporate. Add more zest if needed.

Pour over the crust. Allow to firm in the fridge for at least 8 hours, ideally 12 hours.

YIELD: 6 SERVINGS

Heather Pace's passion for food led her to the completion of a two-year culinary school program at the age of twenty-one. She used her valuable skills and experience to create healthy vegan, and later raw vegan versions of traditional foods. Heather has worked in various restaurants, bakeries, and as a personal chef. She is the author of seven raw dessert e-books, owns a raw dessert and chocolate company, teaches raw food classes, and works as a certified yoga instructor. Find her books and recipes at SweetlyRaw.com. Find her raw chocolates at sweetlyrawchocolate.com.

Stuffed Glazed Pears

Sweet fruit and savory cheese come together for a perfect dessert or appetizer.

3	very ripe pears
½	cup (60 g) "salty" cheese (See recipe on page 140.)
½	cup (60 g) chopped hazelnuts or walnuts
½	cup (120 ml) maple syrup
¼	cup (60 ml) balsamic vinegar

Peel the pears and slice in half. Scoop out the seed cavity of each pear half with a melon baller. Place the pear halves cut side up on a lined dehydrator tray. Put 2 tablespoons (15 g) of the "salty" cheese on each pear and add the chopped walnuts.

In a bowl, whisk together the maple syrup and balsamic vinegar and drizzle half of it over all the pears, saving the other half. Dehydrate the pear halves at about 118°F (48°C) for 1 hour to warm. Drizzle a little of the reserved balsamic and maple syrup over the warmed pears before serving.

YIELD: 6 PEAR HALVES

Caramel Apple Pear Tart

Apples and pears are perfect for fall, and the caramel layer makes this a super sweet treat.

For the Crust

- ½ cup (75 g) almonds
- ½ cup (50 g) walnuts
- ½ cup (40 g) unsweetened shredded dried coconut flakes
- 1½ cups (270 g) dates

For the Caramel

- 1 cup (180 g) dates
- 2 tablespoons (32 g) almond butter
- 1 teaspoon vanilla extract or vanilla powder
- ¾ cup (175 ml) water

For the Cream Filling

- 1 cup (145 g) almonds, soaked overnight and drained
- ½ cup (120 ml) maple syrup
- ¼ cup (60 ml) lemon juice
- ½ cup (120 ml) water, for blending

For the Apple Pear Topping

- ½ cup (120 ml) maple syrup
- 3 tablespoons (45 ml) lemon juice
- 1 teaspoon ground cinnamon
- ½ teaspoon ground ginger
- ¼ cup (25 g) chopped walnuts
- ¼ cup (25 g) chopped pecans
- ¼ cup (45 g) chopped dates
- 2 medium apples, peeled and sliced thinly
- 2 medium pears, peeled and sliced thinly

To make the crust: In a food processor fitted with an "S" blade, process the crust ingredients until they are crumbly and begin to stick together. (Don't over-process.) Pour the crust mix into an 8-inch (17-cm) tart pan with a removable bottom, and press into the bottom and up the sides.

To make the caramel: Place all the caramel ingredients in a small blender and purée until very smooth. Add more water as necessary for blending. When the caramel is finished, spread it evenly in the bottom of the prepared crust. Store the crust in the refrigerator while doing the next steps.

To Make the cream filling: Put all the cream filling ingredients into a food processor fitted with an "S" blade, and process until very smooth. (This may take several minutes.) Scrape down the sides as needed. When the cream filling is very smooth, pour it into the crust on top of the caramel filling and gently spread it evenly.

To make the apple pear topping: In a bowl whisk together the maple syrup, lemon juice, cinnamon, and ginger. Stir in the walnuts, pecans, and dates. Pour over the apple and pear slices and mix until well coated.

Spread the apple pear mix evenly on top of the cream filling layer. This tart is best served immediately. Store any leftovers in a covered container in the refrigerator for up to a few days.

YIELD: ABOUT 10 SERVINGS

chapter

14

> " … But you have no chocolate! I think of that again and again! My dear, how will you ever manage? "
>
> —Madame de Sévigné, French aristocrat

The Chocolate Chapter

Chocolate has been a favorite food since ancient times, with evidence of cacao consumption dating back to 1900 BCE. The Theobroma cacao tree originated in South and Central America and today is cultivated in the equatorial areas of Africa, Southeast Asia, Costa Rica, Columbia, the Caribbean, New Guinea, and Samoa. The Mayans and Aztecs used chocolate in their most sacred ceremonies and made offerings of cacao beans to their deities. In cacao-growing regions of the Aztec empire, citizens were made to pay cacao as a tax.

Unlike commercially available chocolate, which is full of unhealthy ingredients, such as regular dairy milk, refined sugar, and various chemicals and additives, raw chocolate can be good for you. It has healthy amounts of magnesium, copper, potassium, and iron, and it contains a high level of flavonoids. Flavonoids are phytochemicals, or plant chemicals, that fight inflammation, protect cells, and act as antioxidants. Consuming flavonoid-rich foods can reduce the risk of various physical ailments, including heart disease, blood clots, arthritis, inflammation, and cancer.

Chocolate contains about 300 different known chemicals and compounds, including stimulants. Caffeine is present in small amounts. Theobromine, a weak stimulant similar to caffeine, and phenylethylamine are also present. Stimulants increase the activity of neurotransmitters in the parts of the brain devoted to paying attention and staying alert, and so can give a mood and energy boost, but most chocolate will be no more stimulating than a cup or two of coffee. The stimulant chemicals in cacao have also been thought to increase dopamine, adrenaline, and serotonin levels in the brain, which may account for the mood lift many chocolate lovers report.

Cacao contains the minerals magnesium, calcium, iron, zinc, copper, potassium, and manganese, as well as the vitamins A, B_1, B_2, B_3, C, E and pantothenic acid.

The Necessary Ingredients

Cacao paste is made from cacao beans that have been crushed and milled until they become liquid. It comes in blocks that resemble large chocolate bars and is solid at room temperature. Sometimes called cacao liquid, cacao paste is about 55 percent cacao butter and has no sweetener or other ingredients added. It tends to be smooth and will temper (a method of heating and cooling chocolate) well and result in a firm, high-quality product. It is an excellent choice for chocolate bars and candies. It's also handy to have to shave or chop as an addition to ice creams, cereals, trail mixes, and cookies.

Cacao powder is made from cacao beans that have been processed to remove the cacao butter. Because most of the fat has been removed, cacao powder is hydroscopic, which means it will blend well with water. Because of this, it's ideal for smoothies and drinks. Cacao powder can be used to make chocolate bars and candies, but the cacao butter will need to be added back in.

Cacao butter is the pale yellow fat that is extracted from cacao beans. It tastes and smells like cacao. It's a stable fat and full of antioxidants, so it will keep well without becoming rancid for as long as two to five years.

Cacao nibs are crushed bits of fermented and dried cacao beans.

Coconut oil is a saturated vegetable fat that is solid at room temperature. It's often used in raw food chocolate making, although cacao butter will often be the superior choice.

Sweet!

Sweeteners that are appropriate for raw chocolate making include the following:

Coconut palm crystal sugar is a granulated, dry sugar that comes from the coconut palm and is not raw. It's minimally processed, though, and works exceptionally well in chocolate making where a dry sweetener is needed.

Stevia in powdered form can be used as a sweetener or to enhance other sweeteners in any chocolate recipe. Liquid stevia and stevia extract contain water and so cannot be used in chocolate bars or candies, but they work well in recipes such as pie fillings and smoothies.

Agave, maple syrup, and coconut aminos are liquid sweeteners. They cannot be used to make chocolate bars, but they work wonderfully in pie fillings and smoothies.

Flavorings and Additions

Carob powder also comes from a tropical pod; the pulp is dried to make a sweetish, brown powder that is often used as a substitute for cacao. This can be added to any chocolate recipe as a sweet addition that adds another layer of flavor, or in place of some of the cacao powder.

Vanilla pairs very well with chocolate. For bars and tempered chocolate, it's important to use a dry form of vanilla, such as vanilla beans or vanilla powder. (See how to on page 131.) For recipes where water is tolerated, such as smoothies and pie fillings, vanilla extract will also work well.

Flavor oils are wonderful when added to chocolate. Orange oil extract, almond extract, and peppermint oil work very well and add unique and unexpected flavors.

Spices also go well with chocolate. Cayenne and chili were traditionally used by the Mayans in their cacao, and cayenne or chili powder can add a bit of spicy heat to chocolate today. Cumin, chipotle, cardamom, coriander, lime, or lavender can make interesting pairings. Powdered hibiscus tastes a lot like raspberries, and maca powder tastes a bit like malt; either can be used for an even more unexpected flavor.

Sea salt goes exceptionally well with sweet, dark chocolate. Himalayan, black sea salt, and hickory smoked sea salt, and also have unique qualities to add.

Tempering Chocolate

Tempering chocolate is a process of heating, cooling, and reheating chocolate to alter its structure and properties. It's not difficult once mastered, and it makes a great difference in the quality of the final chocolate. It does need to be precise. Think of it as a chemistry experiment.

The fat in cacao butter can form as many as five different types of crystals when it is heated and cooled. Some of the crystals will come together in rigid rows and make a glossy chocolate that will snap when broken and melt at a lower temperature. Other crystals, or a mix of the various kinds, are less stable and result in chocolate that is dull and that may melt at room temperature.

The process of tempering uses heat to produce the desirable crystals that make good chocolate and eliminate the undesirable crystals that produce inferior chocolate. The chocolate is heated up to 115ºF (46ºC), which breaks up any crystals. It is then cooled to 81ºF (27ºC), which will cause type IV and type V crystals to form. The chocolate is then heated again to 88ºF (31ºC), which will eliminate the type IV crystals, leaving only the desirable type V crystals.

Tempered Chocolate

1¼   cups (250 g) coconut palm crystals, finely ground
1   pound (455 g) cacao paste, divided

Begin by grinding the coconut palm crystals into a fine powder using a spice or coffee grinder, or a blender. Then, using a large kitchen knife, chop the block of cacao paste into small chunks and shavings.

Place two-thirds of the cacao paste and the ground coconut palm crystals into a glass or metal bowl that fits into a double boiler or on top of a saucepan. Put enough water in the bottom of the double boiler or the saucepan to come just below the glass or metal bowl when placed on top. Put the water on the stove over medium-high heat until it comes to a boil.

Once the water has come to a boil, remove it from the heat, and place the bowl of chopped cacao paste and ground coconut palm crystals on the top of the saucepan. Stir often until about 90 percent of the cacao paste is melted and the coconut palm crystals are well incorporated. Remove from the saucepan and wipe any moisture off the bottom of the bowl.

Continue stirring until the rest of the cacao paste is melted. Check the temperature with a chocolate thermometer, which can be purchased in the baking section of most large groceries or from cake and candy supply companies, and allow the melted chocolate to reach 115ºF (46ºC). All the crystals in the cacao will be melted.

Place over the hot water again when necessary to increase the temperature. The process needs to be fairly exact, so check often and make sure the chocolate is at the correct temperature.

Add in the reserved cacao paste chunks, and stir in, allowing them to melt. Check the temperature with a chocolate thermometer often, and continue to stir until the melted chocolate has gone down to 81ºF (27ºC). This is where the type IV and V crystals are formed. The two crystals will not make the best chocolate, and the type IV must be eliminated.

Bring the water in the saucepan or double boiler to a boil again. Place the bowl of chocolate over the saucepan or double boiler, stirring frequently, until the temperature of the chocolate has reached 88ºF (31ºC). At this temperature, the type IV crystals are melted, and the type V crystals are all that remain.

The chocolate is tempered and can now be used to make chocolate bars, candy, or dipped items.

YIELD: ABOUT 1½ POUNDS (700 G)

Basic Chocolate Bars

One batch of Tempered Chocolate will make basic but luscious dark chocolate bars that are simple and elegant.

1   batch Tempered Chocolate (See recipe on page 160.)
1   teaspoon vanilla powder (optional)
    (See how-to on page 131.)
    Pinch of salt

Make one batch of the tempered chocolate and hold it at 88ºF (31ºC). Add the vanilla powder and salt to the melted chocolate, and stir well. Pour into rectangular, candy bar–shaped candy molds. Keep the melted chocolate as close to 88ºF (31ºC) as possible until finished pouring. Place the filled molds in the refrigerator for 1 hour to allow the chocolate to completely harden.

When hardened, the chocolate bars can be stored wrapped at room temperature or in the refrigerator for up to 1 week, or in the freezer for up to several months.

YIELD: 1¼ POUNDS (570 G)

Tip

Interesting additions to any basic chocolate bar can include chopped nuts, chopped dates, dried fruit, dried berries, a sprinkle of salt, a dash of spices such as cayenne, chipotle, or cumin, or flavor oils such as orange, almond, or peppermint.

Dark Chocolate Hazelnut Bark

Like in traditional Mayan chocolate making, this dark chocolate bark gets some heat and a wonderfully spicy kick from cayenne.

- **1   batch Tempered Chocolate (See page 160.)**
- **1   teaspoon cayenne powder**
- **   Pinch of salt**
- **½   cup (110 g) chopped raw hazelnuts**

Make one batch of Tempered Chocolate and hold it at 88ºF (31ºC).

Add the cayenne powder and salt, and stir well. Pour the chocolate out onto parchment paper, allowing it to spread out into a puddle that is about ⅛-inch (3 mm) thick. Don't allow it to spread too thin.

Sprinkle the hazelnuts on top of the melted chocolate and lightly press into place. Put the sheet of chocolate into the refrigerator for about 1 hour to harden.

Store any leftovers in an airtight container for up to 1 week at room temperature or in the refrigerator, or up to several months in the freezer.

YIELD: 1½ POUNDS (700 G)

Chocolate Cheesecake with Chocolate Hazelnut Bark

This chocolate cheesecake is creamy and rich, and the addition of a chocolate and buckwheat crust and spicy chocolate bark on the outside makes it downright decadent as well as unique.

For the Crust

- **1 cup (180 g) dates**
- **½ cup (50 g) buckwheat groats, soaked and dried**
- **½ cup (75 g) almonds**
- **¼ cup (30 g) unsweetened shredded dried coconut flakes**
- **¼ cup (30 g) cacao powder**

For the Filling

- **1 cup (145 g) cashews, soaked overnight and drained**
- **½ cup (120 ml) water**
- **2 ripe avocados, chopped**
- **½ cup (60 g) cacao powder**
- **¼ cup (60 g) melted coconut oil**
- **¼ cup (60 ml) agave syrup**
- **¼ cup (60 ml) maple syrup**
- **1 teaspoon vanilla extract**
- **½ teaspoon salt**

For the Chocolate Ganache Glue

- **3 tablespoons (45 g) melted coconut oil**
- **3 tablespoons (45 ml) agave**
- **3 tablespoons (30 g) cacao powder**
- **½ batch chocolate hazelnut bark (See page 163.)**

Line the bottom and sides of a 6- or 8-inch (15 or 17 cm) springform pan with plastic wrap. (This will prevent the filling from seeping out.)

To make the crust: In a food processor fitted with an "S" blade, process the crust ingredients until they are ground and begin to stick together. Pour into the plastic-lined pan and spread evenly on the bottom, pressing into the pan. Place in the freezer while preparing the rest of the recipe.

To make the filling: In the food processor fitted with an "S" blade, process the cashews and water until very smooth and creamy. (This will take a few minutes.) Scrape down the sides of the food processor as needed.

Add the avocados, cacao powder, coconut oil, agave, maple syrup, vanilla, and salt, and process until the entire mixture is very smooth and creamy. Pour into the prepared pie crust and place in the freezer for at least several hours.

To make the chocolate ganache glue: Mix together the coconut oil, agave, and cacao powder. Break the chocolate hazelnut bark into 2-inch (5-cm) shards. Use the chocolate ganache as glue. Place a small blob of ganache on the inside of each chocolate bark shard, and adhere it to the sides of the frozen pie.

Allow the cheesecake to sit at room temperature for about 10 minutes before cutting and serving. Any leftovers can be wrapped in plastic wrap and frozen for up to 1 month.

YIELD: 6 SERVINGS

Tip
A little water on the fingertips will make spreading out sticky pie crusts or cookies a snap.

Raw Mocha Almond Brownie Bites

By Amy Lyons

These delectable little brownies are beautiful but also not too difficult to make, and they're an excellent and decadent dessert.

For the Brownie

- **8** soft Medjool dates, pitted (if not soft, soak them for 30 minutes in filtered water and drain well)
- **2** cups (170 g) finely shredded dried coconut
- **1** cup (100 g) raw almond flour
- **½** cup (80 g) cacao powder
- **¼** cup (60 ml) agave
- **½** teaspoon sea salt
- **1** teaspoon coffee extract
- **1** teaspoon almond extract
- **1** teaspoon vanilla extract

For the Chocolate

- **⅓** cup (25 g) cacao powder
- **½** cup (120 g) melted coconut oil
- **¼** cup (60 ml) agave nectar
- **Pinch of sea salt**
- **½** cup (55 g) chopped raw almonds, for topping

To make the brownie: In a food processer, combine the dates, coconut, almond flour, and cacao powder and process until well blended and the consistency of flour. Add the agave, sea salt, and extracts, and process until smooth and starting to hold together when squeezed. (If it doesn't, add a little more agave nectar.)

Turn out onto a foil-lined sheet pan, and press into a square about 1½-inches (4 cm) thick. Place in the freezer until firm, about 30 minutes. Once firm, cut into 1½-inch (4 cm) squares and place back in the freezer while you make the chocolate.

To make the chocolate: Whisk together all ingredients until smooth. Remove the brownies from the freezer, set the chocolate bowl next to them, and place the chopped almonds in a bowl next to that. Dip each brownie into the chocolate, letting the excess drain off. (I set it on a fork while dipping to allow for that.) Then place it back on the foil, and sprinkle it with some of the chopped almonds. Once the brownies have all been dipped, place them in the freezer to harden (just about 3 to 5 minutes). Enjoy! Extras can be stored in the fridge.

YIELD: MAKES ABOUT 20 BITES

Amy Lyons is the blogger and recipe writer behind Fragrant Vanilla Cake, a blog featuring raw and vegan desserts as well as a few savory dishes. She is also the author of Rawlicious Desserts published in 2013. She graduated from Bethel University in 2007 with a degree in studio art, and she has a passion for creating beautiful things and helping others eat healthier. To learn more about Amy and to see some of her recipes, visit her at fragrantvanillacake.blogspot.com.

Macaroon Hearts Dipped in Chocolate

These easy-to-make, sweet, and crunchy treats are great for every day and also excellent for holidays and special occasions.

1 cup (85 g) unsweetened shredded dried coconut flakes
¾ cup (105 g) almonds
1¾ cups (315 g) dates
¼ cup (60 ml) agave
  Pinch of salt
½ batch Tempered Chocolate (See page 160.)

In a food processor fitted with an "S" blade, process the coconut flakes, almonds, dates, agave, and salt until the ingredients are ground and are sticking together.

Roll out the dough to approximately ¼-inch (6 mm) thick, and then cut into shapes with a cookie cutter. (A heart shape works well, but any shape is fine.) They can also be cut into squares or diamonds with a knife. Place onto unlined dehydrator sheets, and dry at 118°F (48°C) for several hours or overnight.

When the cookies have dried, they will be slightly crunchy on the outside and softer on the inside. Place the cookies on a flat tray or plate, and allow them to chill in the refrigerator for 1 hour. Dip half of each cookie into melted chocolate, place on parchment paper or plastic wrap, and return to the refrigerator until the chocolate has hardened.

Leftovers can be stored in an airtight container for up to 1 week.

YIELD: EIGHTEEN 2-INCH (5-CM) COOKIES

Chocolate Fingerprint Cookies

Chocolate fingerprint cookies are one of my favorites, especially at holidays. This new old favorite is crispy on the outside and has a delectable chocolate chunky center.

For the Cookies

- ¾ cup (75 g) buckwheat groats, soaked and dried
- ¾ cup (105 g) almonds
- ½ cup (40 g) unsweetened shredded dried coconut flakes
- 1½ cups (270 g) dates
- 1 teaspoon vanilla powder
- Pinch of salt

For the Filling

- 6 tablespoons (90ml) coconut oil
- 6 tablespoons (90 ml) agave
- 6 tablespoons (30 g) cacao powder

To make the cookies: In a food processor fitted with an "S" blade, process all the cookie ingredients until they are ground and begin sticking together. Roll the dough out to about ¼-inch (6-mm) thick and cut into 2-inch (2.5 cm) circles. Use a round cookie cutter or a small glass for perfect circles.

Press the center of the cookie with your thumb, leaving a depression. Then place on unlined dehydrator sheets, and dry at 118°F (48°C) for several hours or overnight.

When the cookies are dried, they will be slightly crunchy on the outside and soft on the inside. Cool them by placing them on a flat tray or plate and refrigerating them for 1 hour. They must be fully cooled before putting the filling in them. They will firm more as they cool, as well.

To make the filling: Mix together the filling ingredients. Fill the center depression of each chilled cookie. Place in the refrigerator until the filling is firm.

Store refrigerated in an airtight container for up to 1 week.

YIELD: EIGHTEEN 2-INCH (2.5 CM) COOKIES

Chocolate Mixed Nut Fruit and Seed Clusters

These charming clusters are so delicious and pretty no one would ever guess they're also full of good-for-you flavonoids and antioxidants.

- 1 teaspoon vanilla powder
- 1 teaspoon cayenne powder (optional)
- 1 batch Tempered Chocolate (See page 160.)
- ¼ cup (25 g) chopped almonds, soaked and dried
- ¼ cup (25 g) chopped pecans, soaked and dried
- ¼ cup (25 g) chopped cashews, soaked and dried
- ¼ cup (30 g) shelled sunflower seeds, soaked and dried
- ½ cup (80 g) dried mango
- ½ cup (80 g) dried cherries

Stir the vanilla powder and cayenne powder, if using, into the tempered chocolate, and mix well. Gently fold in the remaining ingredients, stirring just enough to incorporate evenly.

Spoon the mix in mounds about 2 inches (5 cm) across on a sheet of parchment paper. Place them into the refrigerator or freezer to firm for about ½ hour. Allow the clusters to sit at room temperature for 15 minutes before serving.

This recipe makes a fairly large amount of clusters. It's an ideal recipe if taking treats to a holiday or other event where they can be shared with others. Leftovers can be easily stored in a covered container in the refrigerator for up to several weeks.

YIELD: ABOUT THIRTY-TWO 2-INCH (5 CM) CLUSTERS

Raw Berry Cream Brownies

By Emma Potts

These brownies are delightful, and the berry layer is unexpectedly delicious.

For the Brownies

- **1 tablespoon (15 ml) water**
- **½ teaspoon vanilla extract**
- **¼ cup (60 ml) maple syrup or agave (I used 2 tablespoons [28 ml] of each.)**
- **⅓ cup (75 g) unsweetened apple purée**
- **⅓ cup (25 g) raw cacao powder**
- **⅓ cup (40 g) coconut flour**
- **⅓ cup (40 g) almond flour or blanched ground almonds**
- **Pinch of salt**

For the Berry Cream

- **½ cup mixed frozen berries, defrosted or fresh, if in season**
- **¼ cup (35 g) cashews, soaked, rinsed, and drained**
- **1 tablespoon (15 ml) maple syrup**
- **1 teaspoon lemon juice**
- **Pinch of salt**
- **2 tablespoons (30 ml) coconut oil**

Line a small baking tin or container with parchment paper to help remove the brownies (I used a 5½- x 3-inch [14 x 7.6 cm] container).

To make the brownies: In a food processor, combine the water, vanilla, agave, and apple purée.

In a separate bowl, stir together the dry ingredients. Add the dry ingredients to the food processor, and process again until fully incorporated. (You will have a very thick mixture.) Spread the mixture into the prepared container and smooth out the top. Refrigerate.

To make the berry cream: Blend the berries, cashews, maple syrup, lemon juice, and salt. When smooth, add the coconut oil, and blend again.

Pour the berry cream on top of the brownie, and spread evenly across the top. Refrigerate or freeze for a few hours until firm. Use the parchment paper to remove from the container and cut into pieces.

Store in the fridge or freezer because the topping will melt if left at room temperature.

YIELD: 6 BROWNIES

Emma Potts lives in Oxford, England, and is a lover of healthy raw and vegan food. On her blog, she shares her foodie adventures, fun in the kitchen, and explores vegan options in the real world. Learn more about Emma and see some of her recipes at coconutandberries.com.

Freezer Fudge

This is a super-easy, quick, and tasty chocolate treat. A little bit of cayenne adds an unexpected but subtle bit of heat.

⅓	cup (80 ml) coconut oil
⅓	cup (85 g) coconut butter, melted
3	tablespoons (50 g) almond butter
⅔	cup (60 g) cacao powder
⅔	cup (130 g) coconut palm crystals sugar, finely ground
½ to 1	teaspoon cayenne pepper (optional)
¼	teaspoon salt
¼	up (30 g) chopped walnuts
¼	cup (35 g) chopped almonds

In a bowl mix together the coconut oil, coconut butter, almond butter, cacao powder, sugar, cayenne, and salt. Stir until well incorporated and smooth. Pour into a small plastic container that is approximately 6 x 6 inches (15 x 15 cm). Scatter the walnuts and almonds across the top of the fudge before it has hardened. Place in the refrigerator or freezer until firm. Cut apart into squares. Store covered in the freezer for up to 3 months.

YIELD: ABOUT NINE 2-INCH (2.5-CM) SQUARES

Easy Chocolate Sauce

This is a liquid chocolate sauce that goes with just about everything. It's particularly good drizzled over fresh fruit or frozen Banana Ice Cream.

½	cup (120 ml) agave
½	cup (40 g) cacao powder
¼	cup (60 ml) olive oil
¼	teaspoon vanilla extract
¼	teaspoon salt

Whisk together all ingredients and use how you like.

Store leftover sauce in the refrigerator in a sealed container for up to 1 week.

YIELD: ABOUT 1 CUP (235 ML)

Buckeyes

Buckeyes are another traditional favorite that can be enjoyed as a raw treat. They are so named because they resemble the nuts from the Buckeye tree.

- ⅔ cup (130 g) coconut palm crystals sugar, finely ground
- 1 cup (260 g) almond butter
- 1 teaspoon vanilla powder
- ½ batch Tempered Chocolate (See page 160.)

Grind the sugar into a fine powder using a spice or coffee grinder. Mix with the almond butter and vanilla powder until all ingredients are uniformly incorporated into a creamy but somewhat firm dough.

Using a tablespoon to measure out the portions, scoop out the almond butter dough mixture. Roll each portion into a ball, and place on a parchment-covered plate. Place in the refrigerator for 1 hour, until the balls are chilled and firm. Using a toothpick, skewer each chilled ball in the center and dip them about two-thirds deep into the tempered chocolate. Let the majority of extra chocolate drip back into the bowl, and then place the balls, chocolate down, on a parchment-covered plate. Place in the refrigerator for about 1 hour to allow the chocolate to harden.

Store covered or in a lidded container in the refrigerator for up to 1 week, or in the freezer for up to a few months.

YIELD: ABOUT 18 BUCKEYES

Basic Brownie with Chocolate Frosting

Simple, sweet, and chocolaty, this brownie is a new twist on an old favorite and is substantial enough to share with a friend.

For the Brownie

- ½ cup (90 g) dates
- ½ cup (75 g) cashews or almonds
- ¼ cup (20 g) cacao powder
  Pinch of salt

For the Frosting

- 1 tablespoon (15 ml) coconut oil
- 2 tablespoons (30 ml) agave
- 2 tablespoons (10 g) cacao powder

To make the brownie: In a food processor fitted with an "S" blade, process all brownie ingredients until they are ground and begin to stick together. Pour the brownie mix into a rectangular mold and press to firm. A tartlet pan works well, but any small, rectangular-shaped container will do. Press well until the brownie is firm and will hold its shape. Then turn the pan over and release the brownie onto a plate.

To make the frosting: Mix together the frosting ingredients until smooth and creamy. Spread on top of the brownie and enjoy.

YIELD: 1 LARGE BROWNIE

Resources

There is a growing number of resources available that serve those living a raw and vegan lifestyle. Everything from blogs to shops to real-life restaurants can be easily found today. Enjoy these resources where you'll find a number of supplies, information, and services.

Websites, Blogs, and Online Communities

The raw food and vegan community has an active and vibrant online presence. There are many placed to find recipes, lifestyle blogs, and even virtual communities. Try some of these websites for valuable information, recipes, and support.

Raw Food Rehab *www.rawfoodrehab.ning.com*

The World Peace Diet *www.worldpeacediet.org*

Raw Judita Wignall *www.rawjudita.com*

Sweetly Raw *www.sweetlyraw.com*

Fragrant Vanilla Cake *fragrantvanillacake.blogspot.ca/*

Vimergy *vimergy.com*

Betty Rawker *bettyrawker.com/*

The Split Plate *thesplitplate.blogspot.com/*

Coconut and Berries *coconutandberries.com*

Peace Love and Quinoa *www.peacelovequinoa.com*

Rawmazing *www.rawmazing.com*

Healthy. Happy. Life *kblog.lunchboxbunch.com/*

This Rawsome Vegan Life *www.thisrawsomeveganlife.com*

The Simple Veganista *thesimpleveganista.blogspot.ca/*

Manifest Vegan *www.manifestvegan.com/*

Golubka *golubkakitchen.com*

Online Products

The majority of the ingredients in this book will be found at local groceries, but for less commonly available items, like chocolate making supplies or specialty nuts, look to these online resources for quality supplies.

Natural Zing: Cacao, Cacao paste, Sweeteners, Nuts, Dried Fruit *www.naturalzing.com*

Solgar: Acidophilus powder *www.solgar.com*

Raw Guru: Nuts, Seeds, Cacao, Chocolate Supplies, Dried Fruit, Spices, Superfoods, Sea Vegetables *www.rawguru.com*

Nuts.com: Nuts, Dried Fruit *www.nuts.com*

Frontier Natural Food Coop: Nutritional Yeast, Herbs, Spices, Nuts, Teas *www.frontiercoop.com*

Betty Rawker: Nut Milk Bags *bettyrawker.com*

City & Sea Trading Co.: Clothing, Supplements, Oral Care *www.cityandseatrading.com*

Acknowledgments

There is so much for which I'm grateful. I'd especially like to thank my readers, who have been with me through the years. I've enjoyed your support and friendship and hope I've provided useful information, including inside this book, that helps make your life and health journey just a little easier and a lot more delicious.

Thank you to everyone at Quarry Books, who believed in this project from the beginning. Special thanks to Tiffany and John, who were always at the ready with advice and guidance in taking this book from an idea to a reality.

The raw food community is a true joy. Thank you, Penni Shelton, for writing the foreword, your continuing support, and for being such a wonderful leader in the raw and real food community. I'm so grateful to my recipe contributors: Judita Wignall, Heather Pace, Casey McCluskey, Amy Lyons, Jingee Talifero, Emma Potts, Andrea "Betty Rawker" Wycoff, Crista Lash, and Beth Mickens. A special thanks to Judita Wignall, whose encouragement and support has been much appreciated. I'd also like to express my most sincere appreciation for my recipe testers, who let me know what works in real raw kitchens.

Thank you to my family and friends. Thank you to Kevin, who stands by me in good times and bad and weathers every storm without complaint. To my children, Jessica and Michael, and my grandchildren, Alexandria, Ledger, and Carter, thank you for making my life wonderful beyond words. Thank you to my parents, Cliff and Freida, who have always done their best to be there for all of us. Thank you Susan, for being such a great sister and for sharing Noah with me. I love you all.

About the Author

Lisa Viger is a vegan artist, photographer. gardener, food blogger, navel gazer, and lover of the planet and all its inhabitants. More than almost anything, she enjoys showing others that a healthy vegan lifestyle can be economical, simple, fun, and delicious, too. Lisa lives in rural Michigan in a twisty house on a windy hill that sits between a wild creek and a lazy berry patch. She shows readers how to go Raw on $10 a Day at www.rawon10.com.

Index

Note: <u>Underscored</u> page references indicate boxed text. **Boldface** page references indicate photographs.